An Obsession Made In Japan

Fanatic fashion consumption, Otaku and the bubble economy

Takeharu Sato
Fashion Director
takeharusato.com

Copyright © 2020 Takeharu Sato

Contents

Preface **p.6**

Acknowledgements **p.10**

Introduction Japanese Consumption, Kyoichi Tsuzuki's Photography, Otaku Culture

THE ECONOMIC CLIMATE AND CONSUMPTION IN JAPAN SINCE THE LATE 1980s **p.14**

HAPPY VICTIMS – FASHION-OBSESSED PEOPLE DEPICTED BY KYOICHI TSUZUKI FROM 1999 TO 2006 **p.21**

OTAKU CULTURE – REVEALED IN THE LATE 1980s **p.26**

THE METHODOLOGY **p.29**

Chapter One Case Study

ZEN STEREOTYPE **p.41**

TSUZUKI, INTERIORS AND *TOKYO STYLE*
1. Background **p.43**
2. Tsuzuki's photographic style **p.46**
3. Tsuzuki as a pioneer in *Tokyo Style* **p.47**

4. Tsuzuki's influence on young Japanese people **p.48**

HAPPY VICTIMS: KYOICHI TSUZUKI'S PHOTOGRAPHIC SERIES IN *RYUKO TSUSHIN* MAGAZINE
1. The description of *Happy Victims* **p.49**
2. Readership of *Ryuko Tsushin* **p.53**
3. Tsuzuki's photographic style in *Happy Victims* **p.54**
4. Yutaka Ishibashi: Social caste depicted in *Happy Victims* **p.59**

Chapter Two Otaku –
from minority to majority as participatory consumers

WHO IS OTAKU? **p.68**

OTAKU AS PART OF THE JAPANESE MAINSTREAM SINCE THE 1990s; ANALYSIS OF COMIC MARKET **p.72**

FAN CULTURE – A PSYCHOLOGICAL APPROACH **p.76**

THE SIMILARITY OF OTAKU AND HAPPY VICTIMS **p.82**

IS AN OTAKU A COLLECTOR? **p.85**

THE LEGITIMISATION OF COLLECTION **p.89**

THE INTERNET – ONE OF THE PRIMARY SOURCES FOR THE DEVELOPMENT OF OTAKU CULTURE **p.92**

Chapter Three Japanese Homes

BREACHING THE PUBLIC/PRIVATE DISTINCTION **p.99**

A TRADITIONAL ELEMENT INHERITED BY THE MODERN JAPANESE HOME **p.104**

EUROPEAN AND JAPANESE NOTIONS OF PUBLIC/PRIVATE IN THE IDENTIFICATION OF THE SELF **p.107**

THE TRADITIONAL AND MODERN HOME **p.118**

HOME AS A CURATORIAL SPACE **p.123**

THE JAPANESE FAMILY BREAKS DOWN: FROM NUCLEAR FAMILY TO INDIVIDUALS **p.126**

Conclusion The media influences consumption, consumption influences the media

CONSUMPTION REFLECTS PERSONAL IDENTITY **p.135**

A DOUBLE MEANING AND THE UNIFICATION OF TRENDINESS AND OTAKU **p.138**

Interview Records **p.141**

Bibliography **p.157**

Preface

In the summer of 2020, I decided to reedit and publish the MA dissertation I wrote in 2007 for my History of Design course at the Royal College of Art (WARNING: Although, I received a 'good pass', it wasn't a 'distinction'!). Actually, when I first showed this research for my degree show in June 2007, I received queries from a few British publishers who were interested in buying my work. That show was beautifully set in a huge tent in London's Kensington Gardens and ran over the course of two weeks. After that fortnight came to an end, I politely declined the publishers' offers. I thought that, one day, I could publish it myself. That time has now come.

It's been more than a decade since that show, and the world and the way we communicate has changed a lot. In 2019, Japan welcomed its largest ever number of international tourists (31 million people)[1], while the rise of social media platforms such as Instagram has enabled users to share information about Japanese hotspots, fashion and culture both instantly and globally. Social media certainly seems to have boosted Japanese tourism. In 2006, when I was doing my field research, Japan had only 7.3 million visitors. More people than ever have become interested in the country.

My dissertation was completed just before the global proliferation of social media; Facebook had recently begun to become popular, but we could not yet browse the internet on our phones as

---

[1] Japan National Tourism Organization, *https://www.jnto.go.jp/jpn/statistics/since2003_visitor_arrivals.pdf*, (Tokyo: JNTO, accessed 5 August 2020).

easily as now. Throughout my field research, my classmates and I were still heavily dependant on print media to catch up on trends. In this book, I focus on the 1990s-2000s, a time when print media was not only influential, but was actually the only media through which you could catch cool or niche trends – things that were rarely covered by television or radio. Those years also saw the peak in Japan's fashion consumption.

The 1990s in Japan was an interesting period – the nation's 'bubble economy' had ended, but many had not yet woken up from its dream of millions of yen. People still spent a lot of their disposable income on clothes, shoes and bags, often favouring those from a particular fashion brand to which they felt a connection. Many spent as little as possible on their rent in order to save money to buy fashion.

These glamorous, frivolous days did not last forever. In 1997 Yamaichi Securities, one of Japan's four biggest stock brokerage companies, filed for bankruptcy. It was a huge financial scandal and emblematic of the end of Japan's boom years. I was a university student at that time, watching the news on TV, and I could not help thinking that we could no longer trust big corporations. In 1998 I started job-hunting and I can still remember that even Japan's biggest publishing houses were barely hiring. Companies were taking only one or two university graduates, sometimes even zero – a situation that would have been impossible in the 1980s. As even the nation's largest companies began hiring fewer university graduates, Japan entered its 'Employment Ice Age' and, in 2000, one of the country's biggest department stores, SOGO, also filed for bankruptcy – another shock to signal the end of the halcyon days of fashion and lifestyle retail. The Japanese people had finally woken up from their bubble dream.

In 2010, Japan saw its GDP overtaken by China's. For the first time in 42 years, Japan was not the world's second largest economy. Since the 1990s, wages and consumer prices in Japan have changed very little. For a good example of this, try visiting some of its family-run restaurants – you'll soon see that both their menus and prices have remained largely the same for decades. If you were to order a bowl of ramen noodles, it would still cost around ¥600-800 (although it depends on where you go!), a price range that has remained largely fixed since the 1990s. Yet recently the world has experienced catastrophes such as the 2008 economic crisis and the Covid-19 pandemic of 2020. Both at home and internationally, the economic climate is not good. As such, young people in Japan aren't buying clothes as much as they used to.

In this climate, it may be surprising to see quite how crazy young people's consumption in Japan was in the 1990s and 2000s, and how much of it was fuelled by print media and photography. In this book, you should find sources of information that are not available online. Even if millions of visitors have recently begun to experience Japan, you will still find undiscovered parts of the country within these pages. This book is about local people's real life and consumerism – topics that you cannot easily find on your laptop or mobile phone. If you had limited time in Japan, and only visited the tourist hotspots, how else could you find out about this?

I would like to note that, after more than a decade, some of the online sources I referred to in my dissertation, and which I have retained here, are no longer to be found. However, most of my field research consists of interviews, as well as a number of books and magazines in both Japanese and English – sources more permanent and less simple to erase than a webpage.

Acknowledgements

Were it not for many people's kind help, this work could not have been produced. I would like to thank Kyoichi Tsuzuki, who generously accepted my offer for an interview as well as inspiring my theme. I would also like to thank Misho Matsue, the editor of *Ryuko Tsushin* at the time of my field research over the summer of 2006. (Sadly, the magazine was discontinued after its January 2008 issue. This difficult decision must have been made in 2007, shortly after the completion of my dissertation). I wish Matsue well in her current field. Nagi Noda, Seiji Kimura and Yutaka Ishibashi – all three of these interviewees have contributed greatly to this book by giving me their time. I must not forget the people who introduced me to my interviewees; without their help, I would not have been able to contact them. Mieko Kobayashi and Rina Matsunuma, who kindly passed me the contacts of Nagi Noda and Misho Matsue. Keiko Sato, the then-PR of Marc Jacobs, who introduced me to Kimura. Tetsuya Nagata, the fashion stylist who introduced me to Ishibashi having studied at the Bunka Fashion College where Ishibashi taught.

At the Royal College of Art, I was lucky to have the opportunity to learn with excellent supervisors. David Crowley has always led me in the right direction, and particularly in the construction of my overall thesis. Viviana Narotzky especially helped me in my discussion of Japanese homes. I also would like to thank Inge Maria Daniels, who also inspired me to work on this theme. Ulrich Lehmann supported me before this project started, although he moved on to teach at Kent University after our initial discussion of my thesis. I hope he is well.

I also need to thank Hirofumi Kurino, senior adviser for creative direction at United Arrows in Japan and an honorary fellow of the Royal College of Art, who recommended a number of pieces of literatures for my dissertation.

Oli Stratford did great work helping to edit my thesis in order to turn it into a proper book. I appreciate his critical point of view and attention to detail. Without his help, my book would not have been at the same level. And without Johanna Agerman Ross's kind introduction, I would have never met Stratford.

Finally, this work is dedicated to Kinuyo Sato, my mother, who always encouraged me to study at the Royal College of Art and live in London; Haruka, my sister, who takes care of my mother when I am away from Japan; and Kakuya, my father, who is in heaven.

'Tell me what you wear, and I will tell you what your life is like. If you run to an extreme, clothes organise your life as well. When obsessed with a particular brand, his or her living space could be reflected deeply by the design intention of the brand. I would like to travel from one room to another in my series to investigate this hypothesis.'

—Kyoichi Tsuzuki, *Happy Victims*, Volume 1[2]

---

[2] Kyoichi Tsuzuki, *Happy Victims*, Volume 1, *Ryuko Tsushin* (Tokyo: INFAS Publications, April 1999), p.148.

Introduction

Japanese Consumption
Kyoichi Tsuzuki's Photography
Otaku Culture

THE ECONOMIC CLIMATE AND CONSUMPTION IN JAPAN SINCE THE LATE 1980s

From the late 1980s to the late 1990s, Japan experienced an unusual economic period: the 'bubble economy'. During this time, real estate prices rose enormously and general consumption flourished. Restaurants, bars and nightclubs were always packed, while taxi drivers might refuse customers in the street if they did not flash a 10,000 yen note (the highest denomination available) after a night out. Nowadays, people tend to catch the last train home. Empty taxis are everywhere in Japan.

People enjoyed this time – life was good, fickle and frivolous. Historically, it was also a distinctive period. A number of companies, institutions and private individuals invested a huge amount of money in real estate, art, stocks and shares both domestically and internationally. In 1987, Vincent Van Gogh's *Sunflowers* sold for $39.9m at a Christie's auction in London, bought by Tokyo's Yasuda Fire and Marine Insurance Company.[3] In 1989, Mitsubishi Estate bought The Rockefeller Center in New York for about $850m, which seemed symbolic of the period. Investments of these kinds were made possible because of the sharp rise in value of the yen following the Plaza Accord of 1985,[4] an agreement signed at New York's Plaza Hotel between the USA, United Kingdom, France, West Germany and Japan. Its effect was to depreciate

---

[3] '"Sunflowers" Buyer: Japanese Insurer', *https://www.nytimes.com/1987/04/09/arts/sunflowers-buyer-japanese-insurer.html*, (New York, The New York Times, accessed on 14 November 2020).

[4] Hiroyuki Hara, *Theory on Bubble Culture*, (Tokyo: Keio University Publishing, 2006), p.136.

the US dollar in relation to the yen and the German Deutsche Mark by intervening in the currency market.

Meanwhile, in the fashion industry, there was much to discuss. New Japanese designers, such as Comme des Garçons and Yohji Yamamoto achieved commercial and critical success in Paris. These became known as DC Brands (a 'Japanglish' word that stands for 'Designer's & Character's Brands', although it is worth noting that the definition was always vague and the term is no longer used in the 21st century), and also included Men's Bigi and Milk Boy among their number, even if these latter brands never promoted themselves abroad. Thanks to the rising value of the yen brought about by the Plaza Accord, international high-fashion brands became more accessible to Japanese consumers.[5]

The bubble, however, eventually burst. On Monday, 19 October 1987, Dow Jones Industrial Average stock lost almost 22 per cent in a single day – Black Monday – triggering a global stock market decline. By 1991, real estate values were falling too. Many businesses collapsed and swathes of middle-aged employees, those whose experience and skill were invaluable to companies, were either made redundant or else offered shortened working hours as part of a society-wide belt-tightening. In 1991, Japan's actual economic growth rate decreased drastically to 2.9 per cent from 5.5 per cent only a year previously. The following year it fell to 0.4 per cent.[6] The belief that Japanese people could ensure their own welfare by virtue of a job for life vanished. Annual forecasts for

---

[5] Hara, p.136.

[6] Hirohiko Okumura, *Theory on Modern Japanese Economy*, (Tokyo: Toyo Keizai Shinposha, 1990), p.5.

Japan's economy were based on the notion of 3 per cent growth and, when this model went awry, it became difficult for many companies to maintain their seniority system by which full-time workers received automatic promotions and pay rises as they grew older, no matter how skilled they were. This seniority system was the basis for lifetime employment[7] – many employees' life plans would have gone wrong because of changes to these traditional practices.

The seniority system, and the lifetime employment it afforded, had been particularly enjoyed by salarymen – those white-collar, middle-class workers who spend their career in the employ of a single company, having been hired after graduating from university. 'Salaryman' is an evocative and loaded description. It characterises male workers who are loyal to a single employer and live on their monthly salary; who wear dark suits at all times and who are not generally fashion conscious. A salaryman is thought to be constantly exhausted, a consequence of having dedicated themselves to their company. Many of them work late, sometimes into the early hours of the morning, although this has relaxed recently as the economy has slowed. Writing in 2003, James E. Robertson and Nobue Suzuki describe how, from the early 1960s, the image of salarymen, with their stable incomes and guaranteed credibility, came to serve as an ideal symbol of Japan's postwar period:

> From the beginning of Japan's period of high economic growth in the early 1960s, men's roles became portrayed as those of taxpayers and workers, functioning - as 'correct' citizens - as part of a state sponsored patriarchal industrial-capitalist system that place the family in subordinated support of the state. However, from around the time of the eco-

---

[7] Okumura, p.33.

nomic bubble of the late 1980s and its bursting in the early 1990s, salarymen have been portrayed as more independent of companies and with more diverse and individually relative roles.[8]

However, while Robertson and Suzuki assert that 'salarymen have been portrayed as more independent of companies and more diverse' since the late 1980s, this analysis seems skewed given that many employees were made redundant or had no choice but to work for shorter hours under the name of 'company restructuring'.

Those Japanese people who prefer to be 'more independent of companies' are not actually salarymen. Rather, they are members of younger generations, typically between the ages of 20 and 30, who have observed the economic collapse and bankruptcy of the big companies and who no longer trust the system constructed by their fathers' generation of salarymen. Is there any benefit in taking lifetime employment if there is no guarantee that companies will not collapse in the current economic climate? As I go on to describe in Chapter Three, the increase of freelancers called 'Freeter' (a portmanteau of 'Free Arbeiter' – 'Arbeit' is a German word whose original meaning of 'labour' has been adapted in Japan to mean 'part time job') is representative of how young people are subverting the work systems of older generations.

Another important factor is the growing independence of women. In this period, women often preferred to delay marriage, sometimes choosing not to start a family and have children as their mothers had some 30 years prior to them. Robertson and Suzuki point this out:

---

[8] James E. Robertson and Nobue Suzuki, *Men and Masculinities in Contemporary Japan*, (London and New York: Routledge, 2003), p.7.

> For example, the birthrate has fallen yearly and in 1999 was at the historical low of 1.34 (Ministry of Health, Labour and Welfare 2001), shaking the foundations of Japan's bio politics. Much of the blame here has been attributed to 'selfish' women and their resistance to marriage and reproduction. Young women, however, do not want to repeat the affectively deprived and/or economically constrained lives they have witnessed among their mothers, instead choosing late marriage, non-marriage and low birthrates.[9]

I discuss this matter in Chapter Three, and demonstrate that this phenomenon can be accounted for by the better employment opportunities that arose for women in the late 1980s, as well as the increasing liberty available to them through higher education. These young women have seen their mothers' way of life – becoming a full-time housewife after entering into an early marriage and leaving their careers behind – and chosen to proceed differently. Some of their mothers had been forced to give up their dreams of further education or career development because of pressure from their parents to marry young. However, thanks to the economic growth driven by their parents' generation, women living in Japan today are at greater liberty to choose their own education, career, and partners. With the financial backing provided by their parents, young women are able to study at university and live on their own. Following graduation, there are now a far greater number of career options than would have been presented to their mothers only a few decades previously. To these young women, it is easy to see how their mothers' lives may have seemed constrained or boring, and how they may have yearned for freedom from this future.

---

[9] Robertson and Suzuki, p.11.

Robertson and Suzuki explain that 'the post-bubble economy losses, and more, threatens the hegemonic position and prestige of the middle-class male, at the same time, the legacies of the interrelated growth of a service economy and a culture of mass consumption'.[10] This idea of 'consumption' is based on John Clammer's argument in *Contemporary Urban Japan*, where he discusses how consumption reflects class, as well as generational and gender differences.[11]

The economy, Clammer explains, influences not only the way people work and get married, but also their consumption insofar as 'shopping is not simply to acquire things. It is also to purchase identity'.[12] If there are multiple variants of a particular type of consumer good, then a consumer's choice between these types often reflects their sense of self, taste, body image, and social differences. These differences are interwoven with my discussions around Japan's changing society. Clammer argues:

> A lot of middle-aged people [in the 1990s] remember the life with lack of things prior to the bright life nowadays. Fundamentally in a large framework of conservative society, to be able to go shopping, make a choice, and create an alternative identity is remarkable. The sphere of the expanding possibility and the fruit of abundance give us the new prospect - expansion scene - these do not necessarily challenge the sensitivity of Japanese tradition, however they are expanding and re-defin-

---

[10] Robertson and Suzuki, p.10.

[11] John Clammer, *Contemporary Urban Japan*, translated by Kazutaka Hashimoto, Izumi Hotta, Hidehiro Takahashi and Hiroko Yoshimoto (Kyoto: Minerva Publications, 2001), p.29.

[12] Clammer, p.91.

ing it. If this interpretation is correct, Japan has been expressing the unique experience.[13]

Throughout the bubble economy, young Japanese people experienced this new sphere of consumption and 'the expanding possibility and the fruit of abundance' it brought with it – something which their parent's generation, prior to the bubble economy, did not enjoy as much. A much wider range of consumer goods became available; tourism grew, thanks in part to the development of the Shinkansen bullet train; and a huge number of magazines, comic books and TV shows emerged (although the sheer breadth of choices meant that consumers abandoned many). Once goods were consumed, they might be discarded, recycled or forgotten.

In relation to this, Clammer describes 'cosmopolitan consumption', which partly arose thanks to the efficient connectivity of Japan's major railway stations and department stores (many of these stores are owned by the railway companies - Lumine store, for example, is owned by Japan Railways Group, while Hankyu department store is operated by Hankyu Railway).[14] The stores are located just outside of the station's exit and stay open until late, allowing commuters to seamlessly walk into the world of international products on their way home. From the 1990s onwards, young people purchased products (perhaps too many and too often) from either these stores or independent shops, creating their lifestyles and selves through a process of consumption of both international goods and Japan-made products. They might drink Italian

---

[13] Clammer, p.111.

[14] Clammer, *Contemporary Urban Japan*, (Massachusetts: Blackwell Publishers Inc, 1997), p.34.

wine and eat French-style bread while wearing a Japanese designer's clothes, or live in a room whose tatami mats were adorned with Danish furniture while also visiting local Shinto shrines or Buddhist temples. This way of life transformed young people's actions and views into a semiotic code, at the core of which was the self-consciousness of being Japanese by virtue of consuming the world.[15] On the one hand, this style of consumption is a matter of enjoying a blend of Japanese and global aesthetics, and creating a more multi-dimensional lifestyle; on the other, it reinforces 'Japanese-ness' as a distinct phenomena.[16]

HAPPY VICTIMS – FASHION-OBSESSED PEOPLE DEPICTED BY KYOICHI TSUZUKI FROM 1999 TO 2006

Kyoichi Tsuzuki, the photographer, editor and writer of *Happy Victims* in *Ryuko Tsushin* magazine ('Trend Journal' in English) is one of the major primary sources of this book. Tsuzuki started his career as a journalist for the culture magazines *Brutus* and *Popeye,* where he covered contemporary art, architecture and city life. From the late 1980s, he was involved in the design and spatial concepts behind Tokyo nightclubs such as Gold and Milk, which became emblematic of the bubble period, as well as continuing to write and edit art and design publications. He published his first photographic book *Tokyo Style* in 1993 (this will be introduced properly in Chapter One) and won the 23rd Kimura Ihei Com-

---

[15] Clammer, p.131.

[16] Clammer, p.137.

memorative Photography Award for his later work *Roadside Japan*, which was published in 1996. Ihei Kimura, whom the award is named after, pioneered the use of the Leica camera in Japan prior to World War II and 'was known for snapshot spontaneity in his portraits as well as his photojournalistic work. The award is a major prize for young photographers, it has been awarded wisely, and many of its recipients have gone on to careers of distinction'.[17] As I introduce in Chapter One, this is a close fit for Tsuzuki's photographic style.

Ryuko Tsushin featured Tsuzuki's photographs alongside an accompanying text describing their subject's involvement with fashion. I have interviewed Tsuzuki; Misho Matsue, an editor of *Ryuko Tsushin*; and three people who appeared in Tsuzuki's work and subscribe to the *Happy Victims* lifestyle. I also focus on Japanese and English literature in the disciplines of sociology, consumption studies, and design history, as well as the field of psychology to inform my methodology.

The reasoning behind interviewing these subjects should be clarified. My primary concern is to take an ethnographical approach to Tsuzuki's photography series. In this respect, I hope to make comparisons between the series' subjects, and to analyse the interviews that I conducted in light of secondary sources. I additionally visited the spaces of my three interviewees, allowing me to observe their living/working conditions both inside and outside the home.

---

[17] Anne Wilkes Tucker, 'Why So Personal?' in *Setting Sun,* edited by Ivan Vartanian, Akihiro Hatanaka and Yutaka Kambayashi, (New York: Aperture Foundation books, 2006), p.15.

My aim has been to understand what lies behind Tsuzuki's photographs. Tsuzuki captured his subjects in their rooms and it is worth analysing how people spend their life in these spaces. How, for instance, do they distinguish public from private once they have been published in a magazine; or how do they legitimise living alone, without having a defined role within a traditional family structure? Why did they become obsessed with a single brand, rather than following a wide range of fashion houses? Why did they decide to agree to being photographed by Tsuzuki? Focusing on these questions entails analysing moments that lie outside of the photographs. I have a particular interest, for instance, in reading these phenomena in light of wider patterns of fashion consumption in Japan since the late 1980s.

It is also worth investigating Otaku culture in relation to Tsuzuki's subjects' fashion obsession – the two phenomena may coexist. Otaku culture emerged in Japan in the 1980s and is now mainstream, describing the way that people may obsess over fields such as animation and comic books – fields which have subsequently flourished in accordance with the internet revolution that began to emerge in the mid-1990s. Today, Otaku culture is global thanks to the proliferation of the internet and social media. When I spoke with Tsuzuki's subjects, I asked them questions such as 'Do you recognise yourself as an Otaku?' and 'Are you really happy with your living conditions?', so as to try and connect their answers to broader phenomena within Japanese society. The 1980-90s, the bubble economy, obsessive fashion consumption, Otaku culture – it may not be a coincidence that all of these things happened almost simultaneously.

Through conducting interviews with Tsuzuki's subjects, I was able to understand the reasons behind their obsessions, as well as how they themselves perceive their situation. I also examine the nature of their homes and how this is connected to the fashion items they purchase: what kind of relationship do they have with their rooms and fashion collections, and how do they utilise their small, 'modern', rented spaces? This question involved visiting the spaces myself to make a comparison with traditional detached Japanese houses.

Tsuzuki's photographs are mysterious: most of the subjects of the first 20 volumes were not photographed and their rooms were shot statically without their inhabitants. After those first volumes, readers were normally shown the inhabitant in their space. The reason for this is not complicated. Tsuzuki explained during my interview that even though he had wanted to show the inhabitants from the first volume, the magazine's editor had not. After volume 20, a new editor came in who agreed with Tsuzuki.[18] Even when you can see the inhabitant, the majority are blurred thanks to a long exposure. To me, the work seems semi-voyeuristic or it represents a semi-invasion of privacy. Although the inhabitants had agreed to allow themselves, their fashion collections, and their rooms to be published, they still seem reluctant or shy to disclose their identities – despite the fact that they must have been so proud of their collections! I was keen to know why Tsuzuki had chosen to photograph them in this way.

Happy Victims seemed reminiscent of Tsuzuki's earlier book *Tokyo Style*, which comprises photographs of 100 young, creative,

---

[18] Kyoichi Tsuzuki, personal interview, (Tokyo, 8 September 2006).

Japanese people's rooms, shot over the course of two years. In its depiction of spaces, *Tokyo Style* was the forerunner of Tsuzuki's work for *Ryuko Tsushin*, which shows not only its subjects' fashion collections, but also their interior spaces, replete with tables, chairs, posters or action figures. These are photographs that seem to show us their subjects' character or wider life. Most of the inhabitants are anonymous, yet they somehow still display their identity.

The *Happy Victims* photographs intrigued me, triggering multiple questions. What do these individuals acquire through purchasing high fashion clothes (although not every single Happy Victim was a high-fashion consumer: the series also featured a man obsessed with Nike, a woman obsessed with X-girl, and another woman with the Japanese brand Alba Rosa)? What do they hope to project by exposing their private domestic spaces in this way? Are their spaces private anymore? How do the inhabitants distinguish their private and public space? Is it possible to call them collectors? Or fashion Otaku? Or fashion victims? What kind of message does Tsuzuki want to deliver to the viewer through his photographs? Are the subjects narcissists? Can they even wear all of their fashion items, having purchased so many? How different are they from other kinds of consumers? How legitimate is this type of collecting compared to other forms, such as art?

Here, I would like to quote Susan Sontag's *Where The Stress Falls*. In her chapter 'The Pleasure of the Image', Sontag writes about viewing a painting by the 17th-century Dutch artist Gerard Houckgeest and relates this to how photography inspires us beyond what we actually see in an image:

> Houckgeest's viewpoint is a way of referring to, making the viewer aware of, the much larger space that continues beyond the space depicted within the borders of the picture. This is the method central to the aesthetics of photography (both still photography and film): to make what is not visible, what lies just outside the visual field, a constituent - dramatically, logically - of what we see.[19]

Tsuzuki's photography is not a freak show – 'what lies just outside the visual field' of his photographs is enormous and naturally leads me to analyse that 'much larger space' of Japan's economic rise and fall; the crazy consumerism of Japanese youth in conjunction with the economy of the 1990s; a potential connection between fashion consumption and Otaku culture; and self-identification with a particular fashion brand.

OTAKU CULTURE – REVEALED IN THE LATE 1980s

During the bubble economy, Otaku culture began to become visible. An Otaku is a person who is obsessed with a particular type of consumer goods, be it animation, cartoons, comics, science fiction or personal computers. Amongst scholars and writers who have worked on the subject of Otaku, such as Eiji Otsuka and Hiroki Azuma, it is generally agreed that the term emerged in 1983, when it appeared in the June issue of the comic magazine *Manga Brikko*.[20]

---

[19] Susan Sontag, *Where The Stress Falls*, (London: Jonathan Cape, 2002), p.144.

[20] Eiji Otsuka, *History of Otaku's Spirit: theory on the 1980s*, (Tokyo: Kodansha, 2004), p.16.

Otaku became highly visible in a negative sense, however, as the result of a series of brutal murders that occurred between 1988 and 1989, and which shook Japan. Tsutomu Miyazaki, a serial killer, murdered four young girls before being arrested on 11 August 1989. His small room was found to be filled with several thousand pornographic videotapes, while the floor was covered with a futon that served as a permanently unmade bed. Footage of this apartment was broadcast on TV, while details were published in magazines and newspapers.[21] Miyazaki also possessed an extensive collection of anime and horror videotapes, which caused a moral panic against Otaku and led many in Japan to believe that Miyazaki's crimes had been influenced by his collection. Otaku thus came to the attention of wider Japanese society and began to carry negative connotations of perversion and anti-social behaviour. As Azuma states, 'right after the Miyazaki murder, *Weekly Yomiuri* on the 10th of September 1989 explained that Otaku were not good at communication that was intrinsic for humans and introverts'.[22]

Even with these negative connotations, Otaku culture began to expand during this period, aided by the vast development of Japan's technology industry that saw the rise of personal computers and computer game software. In the early 1980s, the first generation of Japanese-made computers such as the NEC PG-8001, Sharp Z80 and the Fujitsu FM-8 began to be consumed by PC enthusiasts who enjoyed programming their own games using BASIC lan-

---

[21] Otsuka, p.74.

[22] Hiroki Azuma, *Animalising Post-Modern: Japanese Society perceived by Otaku*, (Tokyo: Kodansha, 2001), p.10.

guage or with programmes published in magazines such as *Ascii* and *Log In*. The quality of games improved dramatically in accordance with the development of hardware. In the late 1980s, Fujitsu's FM-Towns computer appeared on the Japanese computer market, and its later *Sim Town* software (made in the USA) featured splendid graphics and sound. This improvement in technology made it impossible for amateurs to self-produce equivalent games as they had in the early 1980s. As such, they became consumers of ready-made software packages.[23]

Otaku culture is still evolving today. Otaku are participatory consumers – they consume animation, cartoons and computer games, but they also produce new things based on those officially sold consumer goods. As I address in Chapter Two, Tokyo hosts a gigantic three-day event called Comic Market twice a year, which around 12,000 people visit each day. This is the place where Otaku and the companies that produce Otaku consumer goods each set up stands to display and sell new products such as comics, posters and action figures. The event is a useful forum insofar as it allows Otaku to share their knowledge about consumer goods through face-to-face communication, as well as making friends with common interests. Another significant forum for Otaku is, of course, the internet. In the mid-1990s, the internet began to expand in Japan, representing a historic milestone for Otaku who had been investigating computers intensively since the 1980s.

---

[23] Hara, pp. 127-128.

THE METHODOLOGY

In order to provide answers to the questions I have raised, this book is divided into three chapters. Chapter One addresses the historical context to Tsuzuki's photography since *Tokyo Style* (1993), a work that was completely set against the minimalist Japanese aesthetic that had been long appreciated by Western scholars such as Suzanne Slesin, Stafford Cliff and Daniel Rozenstroch.

The final part of Chapter One investigates a case study. Yutaka Ishibashi, a fashion teacher at the time of my field research, has been obsessed with the menswear line Maison Martin Margiela ⑩ for more than a decade and is a VIP client of the brand's shop. Ishibashi was featured in *Happy Victims* in 2003 and wears Margiela from head to toe, every day. He cares meticulously for his clothes and shoes so as not to damage the Margiela items. He neither eats, nor drinks in his room in an attempt to ensure cleanliness, a pursuit which he equates with the preservation of his clothes and shoes. I was intrigued by Ishibashi when I read about him and wanted to ask him many questions. Why only Margiela, even if Margiela was a great fashion designer? Why did Ishibashi want to brand himself in that way? Why was he such a perfectionist at preserving his clothes and shoes, given that if you wear them they are extremely likely to become damaged or stained anyway? I managed to interview him in summer 2006, which was a useful source for my research insofar as it relates discussions around the notion of public and private in Japanese homes to an analysis of Otaku culture in comparison with fashion-obsessed individuals.

Chapter Two discusses Otaku culture. The reason behind constructing this section as a separate chapter is because of similarities between Otaku and those who featured in Tsuzuki's series. Although the products they consume are different, their consumption habits are similar. Both Otaku and Happy Victims are participatory consumers inasmuch as they create a new lifestyle or objects based on officially sold products: that is, textual production via the internet (online forums on which people can write comments and exchange knowledge); new comics and products (sold at Comic Market, which appears again in Chapter Two); or even new fashion collections, like those created by one of my fashion heroes, Daiki Suzuki of Engineered Garments – an avid vintage clothing collector and self-taught designer whom I admire for his extensive knowledge of garments and fabrics. Otaku and Happy Victims alike share information and knowledge online, as well as at shops and live events.

At the outset of this section, I use *Research On Otaku Market* by the Nomura Research Institute to organise the various definitions of Otaku. This institute was established in 1965 as the first private think-tank in Japan, and has consulted for Japanese companies on marketing strategies as well as system developments based on its analysis of societal paradigms.

One of these definitions leads to John Fiske's text 'The Cultural Economy of Fandom'. Otaku invest exclusively in their favourite consumer goods and Fiske's work links to this, inasmuch as he argues that investing money results in cultural 'distinction'.[24] Through their investment, Otaku educate themselves in their chosen field.

---

[24] John Fiske, 'The Cultural Economy of Fandom' in *The Adoring Audience: Fan Culture and Popular Media*, edited by Lisa A. Lewis, (London: Routledge, 1992), pp.30-47.

Another field of research arises from Fiske's argument. In December 2006 I attended Tokyo's Comic Market, observing how it enables Otaku to display their newly created action figures and cartoons. Comic Market is hosted at the Tokyo Big Sight, a gigantic events space which has a capacity of 12,000 people. The event was divided into Company (official) and Individual (unofficial). This is reminiscent of Fiske's argument around self-investment, by which Otaku educate themselves. Individual culture has huge potential to become 'official culture', and Comic Market legitimises Otaku culture by bringing it into the public domain. In fact, some manga artists have been discovered by publishers when showing in the Individual section of the event. They have later made their 'official' debut in the Company section.

This area of research incorporates Joli Jenson's psychoanalytical text 'Fandom as Pathology', which asserts that fandom transcends the borderline of 'normal' and 'abnormal'. Fans discriminate between what 'we' (the fans) do as being 'normal' and safe, and what 'they' do as being 'abnormal' and dangerous.[25] The more that fans become obsessed with a certain field, the less they can control their interest and the more they might consider those who do not understand their passion or criticise them as a kind of 'enemy' or distraction (of course, this is only true in the abstract – it is certainly not true of every fan). By applying this idea to my interview with Ishibashi, I could analyse the way in which he distinguished himself from other Otaku. As the interview shows, he exhibited a slight resistance towards being seen as an Otaku.

---

[25] Joli Jenson, 'Fandom as Pathology' in *The Adoring Audience: Fan Culture and Popular Media*, edited by Lisa A. Lewis, (London: Routledge, 1992), pp.9-43.

Chapter Two continues to make comparisons between the ideas of Otaku and collectors. I adopt Jean Baudrillard's text 'The System of Collecting', as well as Russell W. Belk's ideas in his work *Collecting In A Consumer Society*, to define the form of consumption through collecting. Baudrillard states that a collection is enjoyable in other people's eyes with a 'jealousy complex' at an 'innocent level'.[26] We can be jealous of someone who possesses an object you aspire to own. That object may be a car by Aston Martin, a Birkin bag by Hermès, or a screen print by Andy Warhol. This jealousy is not hostile towards the owner of the object, but rather a complex form of admiration – perhaps you cannot afford the object or, if it's a seasonal fashion item, maybe you simply missed the chance to purchase it. These feelings – 'I wish I could afford it' or 'I wish I had known it was out' – can be innocent. Belk, meanwhile, asserts that collecting is a different form of consumption because it involves the acquisition of objects that are not in everyday use. This also functions as a 'display of wealth'.[27]

Otaku and fashion consumption have something in common with these notions. Otaku collect their favourite animation goods, action figures and comics – products that often see their value sharply rise once they are out of print or production. Similarly, seasonal fashion items are often difficult to find once the initial opportunity to buy them has been missed. Therefore, the act of displaying these products can trigger Baudrillard's 'jealousy complex' in

---

[26] Jean Baudrillard, 'The System of Collecting' translated by Roger Cardinal in *The Cultures of Collecting*, edited by John Elsner and Roger Cardinal, (London: Reaktion Books, 1994), p.18.

[27] Russell W. Belk, *Collecting In A Consumer Society*, edited by Susan M. Pearce (London: Routledge, 1995), pp.25-67.

others. However, most of the Happy Victims' fashion products are still in use – they are not purely purchased for 'the display of wealth' as an art collection may be (although, for example, carrying a Hermès Birkin bag or driving an Aston Martin car may be a mobile display of wealth). There is a certain 'grey zone' that exists between Otaku and collectors.

I also focus on the legitimisation of collecting and aim to address the problem of how legitimate Otaku and Happy Victims' collections are compared to other types, such as art and books. I adopt Pierre Bourdieu's concepts for this discussion. Bourdieu (a French structuralist), in his book *Distinction*, argues that art and books are inherited from the past and deposited in museums and private collections, as well as being the product of history accumulated in the form of books, articles, documents and instruments.[28] These historical objects are, therefore, available to a limited number of people to purchase (although they may be available for the public to view), whereas Otaku consumer goods or fashion items do not possess this historical depth – yet.

In the last part of Chapter Two, I address the role which the internet has played in the development of Otaku culture since the late 1990s. One example is the website *Ni Channel* ('Channel Two' in English), which launched in 1999 as an anonymous text board for a wide range of genres. To use Fiske's terminology, *Ni Channel* is where 'textual production' occurs, a forum for millions of anonymous people to share information and knowledge. Daniel Miller and Don Slater's *The Internet: An Ethnographic Approach* is useful in discussing the manner in which the internet has blurred

---

[28] Pierre Bourdieu, *Distinction*, (Massachusetts, Harvard University Press, 1984), p.228.

the boundaries between 'virtuality' and 'reality'. Miller and Slater base their discussion around the use of the internet in Trinidad,[29] but it can also be applied to Japan. It is no longer a matter of being real or unreal – the internet simply is part of our everyday communication.

Chapter Three challenges various notions of the Japanese home. The first two sections address seemingly oppositional ideas – public and private, traditional and modern. In his essay 'Home: The Promise and Predicament of Private Life at the End of the Twentieth Century', Krishan Kumar defines these notion of public and private, although further references are required insofar as Kumar's argument focuses on Europe rather than the East, as well as completely segregating the public and private.

Viviana Narotzky's text 'Dream Homes and DIY: television, new media and the domestic makeover' and Roland Barthes's *Camera Lucida* are useful sources to contrast with Kumar's argument. In her essay, Narotzky uses the example of the domestic makeover TV show *Changing Rooms*, which ran from 1996 to 2004 on BBC1, to discuss how far the boundaries of public and private spaces have been breached through private spaces having been exposed to the public on television. *Changing Rooms*, and programmes like it, were intended for those who enjoy the 'pleasure of looking' into private spaces and Narotzky also suggests that domestic decoration expresses the inhabitant's taste: that is to say,

---

[29] Daniel Miller and Don Slater, *The Internet: An Ethnographic Approach*, (Oxford: Berg, 2000), pp.1-18.

what they do and what they like.[30] This is related to their expression of the 'social role' in domestic spaces that is performed by the inhabitants in *Happy Victims*. Barthes addresses this same point, arguing that there was an implosion of the private following the onset of photography which had the potential to be consumed publicly.[31] These two references support my argument that media forms such as photography reveal the private as public and, as a result, that modern society has blurred the boundaries between what is public and private.

With regard to these blurring boundaries, I focus on Christena E. Nippert-Eng's *Home and Work*, as well as the case study of Nagi Noda, who was featured in *Happy Victims* and whom I interviewed in Tokyo. Both sources are useful to support my argument that the boundaries of public and private can be transcended based on an inhabitant's lifestyle. Noda was an internationally renowned artist, who transcended the boundary of home and work, and expressed her 'outside social role' in her private space. The photo of her in *Happy Victims* looks as if she is using her living room as a stage to confidently display her luxury consumption and occupation.

This discussion leads me to Ervin Goffman's book *The Presentation of Self in Everyday Life*. Goffman notes that we always perform ourselves within social interactions and that our perfor-

---

[30] Viviana Narotzky, 'Dream Homes and DIY: television, new media and the domestic makeover' in *Imagined Interiors*, edited by Jeremy Aynsley and Charlotte Grant, (London: V&A Publications, 2006), pp.258-271.

[31] Roland Barthes, *Camera Lucida*, translated by Richard Howard, (London: Jonathan Cape, 1982), p.98.

mance always depends on the setting.[32] In conjunction with my case study, home is the 'setting' in which to conduct a performance. Noda was by no means an ordinary consumer – she was a successful artist with greater means than the average workers – but Goffman's idea of 'setting' could be applied to all the Happy Victims, who revealed both their private spaces and themselves as subjects of Tsuzuki's photographs.

The second section of Chapter Three focuses on traditional and modern homes. Inge Maria Daniels's text 'The Untidy Japanese House' shows two case studies of families who inhabit detached houses in Japan. One has a traditional Japanese house combined with a modern element (their adjunct house had been turned into an annex for their children), while the other has a recently built property that nevertheless contains a traditional tatami room. Both families follow the traditional Japanese style in terms of the family members' roles in their domestic spaces, as well as their preservation of objects (gifts or heirlooms) in a fashion that appears cluttered.[33] Daniels's discussion of these cluttered domestic objects supports the evidence provided in Tsuzuki's photographs of the clutter in real young people's rooms, as opposed to the minimalism espoused by the European scholars I mentioned earlier.

Pierre Bourdieu's *Distinction* is another useful source for discussing consumption in the home. Bourdieu mapped the distinctions of people in different classes based on ideas of the 'Habitus': the differentiation of their education, occupation and consumption

---

[32] Erving Goffman, *The Presentation of Self in Everyday Life* (New York: Penguin Books, 1990), pp.17-33.

[33] Inge Maria Daniels, 'The Untidy Japanese House' in *Home Possessions*, edited by Daniel Miller, (New York: Berg, 2001), p.204-216.

in the social structure.[34] Although Bourdieu's argument illustrates social classes in France in the 1980s, it is adaptable to Japanese class-differentiation in home consumption, which is described by Daniels.

When I adapt Bourdieu's conception of the Habitus to discuss Ishibashi's home and his consumption of Margiela's items, his differentiation could be seen as the way in which he accumulates and meticulously cares for and displays these clothes and shoes. Ishibashi's room may be interpreted as a Margiela archive. To highlight this point, I use Igor Kopytoff's 'The Cultural Biography of Things: Commoditization as a Process', in which he demonstrates the idea of 'future collectibles'.[35] Mundane objects are able to acquire market value, or later be accommodated in a museum, due to their singularity and rarity.

The final section of Chapter Three suggests that Japanese families have been experiencing a breakdown from a nuclear core to a series of individual cores since the late 1980s. Of the roughly 90 people captured in Tsuzuki's photographs, 80 were single. Needless to say, this is only a tiny sample of Tokyo, although I have thought that it may have something to do with Japan's low birthrate observed in the 1990s.[36] The literature that supports this assumption comes in the form of Gordon Mathew and Bruce White's 'Changing Generations in Japanese Society', Lynne

---

[34] Bourdieu, pp.169-241.

[35] Igor Kopytoff, 'The Cultural Biography of Things: Commoditization as Process' in *The Social Life of Things*, edited by Arjun Appadurai, (New York: Cambridge University Press, 1986), pp.64-81.

[36] Robertson and Suzuki, p.11.

Nakano and Moeko Wagatsuma's 'Mothers and Unmarried Daughters', and Merry White's 'Women and Social Change in Japan'. All these texts discuss the social and economic changes, and shifts in education and employment (particularly for women) that have been influential for postwar Japanese families.

The images in *Ryuko Tsushin* are a small universe – selecting this particular photographic series is a profitable method for analysing modern Japanese society. We can approach the problems of photography; obsessive youth and their mentality; fashion industry and consumption practice; and material culture in Japanese dwellings in conjunction with the notion of public and private, all from this single body of work.

Yutaka Ishibashi in his apartment (Tokyo, September 2006). Ishibashi is dressed in Martin Margiela, and preserves all of his Margiela clothes and bags meticulously. There is not a single speck of dust on the floor.

Chapter One
Case Study

ZEN STEREOTYPE

Japanese architecture and domestics interior have long been appreciated in both their traditional and modern minimalist manifestations. European scholars such as Suzanne Slesin, Stafford Cliff and Daniel Rozensztroch have praised the minimalist interiors of contemporary Japanese houses, co-editing the 1987 book *Japanese Style*, in which they seek to illustrate the 'tug-of-war between traditionalism and modernism, between the East and the West'. Most pre-war, traditional Japanese homes are now gone – the result of a combination of factors such as the renovation of cities, a doubled national population, and rising land values. Combined with this loss is the fact that, since the 1950s, Japanese architecture has been highly influenced by the West.[37] Although the argument set out in *Japanese Style* is useful, the following acknowledgment of its provenance is worth the attention of Western audiences interested in the Japanese home:

> Japan is a country that has long had appeal to foreigners, and modernists in the West have been greatly influenced by the traditional Japanese way of life. Simplicity, functionalism, and minimalism - three of the most important elements of Japanese design - have been appreciated, since the 19th century, and reinterpreted by Western designers and architects... At the outset, we obtained the help of a number of people - journalists, architects, artists, and fashion designers, as well as interpreters, marketing and advertising executives...[38]

---

[37] Suzanne Slesin, Cliff Stafford and Daniel Rozensztroch, *Japanese Style*, (New York: Clarkson N. Potter Inc., 1987), p.2.

[38] Slien, Cliff and Rozensztroch, p.1.

Figure 1: Front cover of *Tokyo Style*.

The minimalist Japanese domestic architecture and interiors of the 1980s are beautifully decorated, and mainly found in Tokyo and its suburbs. However, the authors' analysis concentrates on the work of architects and designers, and does not document how people actually live in these spaces – something that is equally important. As the quotation acknowledges, *Japanese Style* is based on collaborations with those working in the creative industries; it is entirely possible that the homes depicted were either selected for their minimalist aesthetics, or else were somewhat dressed this way in order to help secure healthy book sales – not that there is anything wrong with being successful! The identities of some of the inhabitants of these minimalist rooms are disclosed: successful and wealthy creatives such as the fashion designer Junko Koshino and the stylist Michiko Kitamura. The majority of Japanese people, however, would not have been able to afford this type of space – these rooms would have been reserved for the elite of Japanese society. *Japanese Style* was published in 1987, six years before Tsuzuki's *Tokyo Style*, which offered a counter-presentation and a different approach to looking at Japanese interiors.

TSUZUKI, INTERIORS AND *TOKYO STYLE*

1. Background

Tsuzuki's *Happy Victims* began in 1999 and adopted the same approach that he had pioneered with *Tokyo Style* (1993). This earlier book contains photographs of 100 small and cluttered apartments, the homes of young creative people. It reveals the living arrangements of art school students, aspiring musicians, amateur surfers and graphic designers, none of whom were wealthy at that time.

As the forerunner to *Happy Victims*, *Tokyo Style* requires context. According to an interview with Tsuzuki in the book *Be A Photographer!* by Sayuri Toki:

> The front cover is the photograph (Figure 1) of the room presumably for 30,000 to 40,000 yen monthly for rent. The inhabitant is an aspiring rock musician and roadside worker. It is important for both him and us to think about whether he sings folk songs with a kind of sadness or if he really enjoys his living condition. It would be mentally different if

he thinks positively that he only should work to earn just 35,000 yen. I have wanted to publish the book to tell people that we should live our lives by concentrating on whatever we like, whatever we can enjoy.[39]

Tokyo Style became very popular in Japan, despite its high price of 12,000 yen.[40] An English edition was later published, selling approximately 10,000 copies in the United States, Europe and United Kingdom. Tsuzuki's book was successful because it showed ordinary interiors. Its spaces were chaotic with the clutter and mess of a young Japanese person's life, while brief descriptions of its subjects' lifestyles were set out in the accompanying texts. The book challenged the stereotypical idea held by Western architects and designers that Japanese interiors were predominantly minimalist and Zen in character. Tsuzuki said the following about contemporary Japanese interiors in his introduction to the book:

> Bookstore shelves are lined up with more publications on 'Japanese space' than you would ever want to see. Glossy coffee-table books on the heights of the Japanese aesthetic tradition, whole series of large-format monographs on 'neo-Zen' contemporary architecture, interior décor magazines with full-colour coverages of minimal-chic rooms that stylists have fussed over. But how many of these places look lived-in? That's because what these books show are the co-creations of known architects and photographers, or else very skilful presentations of designer products… On the other hand, I know lots of people who manage to live in cluttered closet-sized walk-ups with great ease and style… Let's put an end to this media trickery, giving poor ignorant foreigners only images of the most beautiful Japanese apartments to drool over. Hence this book: I wanted to show you the real *Tokyo Style*,

---

[39] Sayuri Toki, *Be A Photographer!*, (Tokyo: Metalogue, 1998), p.130.

[40] Toki, p.128.

the places we honest-and-truly do spend our days. Call it pathetically over-crowded, call it hopelessly chaotic... that's the reality.[41]

Figure 2: A tatami room with DJ decks, records and academic books featured in *Tokyo Style*.

These remarks indicate Tsuzuki's philosophy of 'real' Japanese contemporary homes. His photography documents the reality of young people's living conditions in Tokyo, investigating a side of contemporary society which had never previously been studied in depth. This pioneering approach, and Tsuzuki's self-taught and idiosyncratic photographic style, goes some way to explaining why the book became so successful. *Tokyo Style* was striking not only to a Japanese audience, but also to international readers who had previously understood Japanese architecture and domestic spaces through the lens of either traditional Japanese architecture or else

---

[41] Kyoichi Tsuzuki, *Tokyo Style*, translated by Alfred Birnbaum, (Kyoto: Kyoto Shoin, 1993), p.19.

stereotypical minimalism. Tsuzuki's project gave hope to young Japanese people who felt disconnected from the luxurious interiors depicted in fashion and interior magazines such as *Vogue Living* and *Elle Decor*.

2. Tsuzuki's photographic style

Tsuzuki had never taken photographs properly before embarking on *Tokyo Style* and, although he had a clear idea about what he wanted to do, he had a limited budget. As such, he sought advice from professional photographers about which camera might be best for a beginner. Having purchased a Linhof camera, he started the project on his own.[42] This explains why many of Tsuzuki's photographs do not look professional, but rather reveal the hand of an amateur. Although the frames are all well-focused, some nevertheless reveal their amateurism. In Figure 2, for instance, the right corner of the photograph is dark (especially the speaker), while the top side of the frame is bright with daylight – a shift that reveals the exposure was a bit long (although I, for one, am fond of this effect).

As Tsuzuki notes in *Be A Photographer!*, he was proud of his status as a beginner and took advantage of it. 'It is very difficult to arrange a photo shoot in small houses,' he says. 'A professional photographer discouraged me when I was trying to buy some strobe lights, because the small rooms do not have the electricity capacity and sockets to use those (the multiple outlet extension cables should be plugged)… Some professionals make fun of me but it is good enough as long as I can take the photos I need. That

---

[42] Toki, p.122.

is why I do not need any complicated techniques'.[43] This amateur, snapshot style of photography revealed the everyday life of ordinary Japanese people; published in a book for the first time, it was a marked contrast to the perfection and glamour of most professional photographers' work, and the highly designed and styled spaces they typically shot.

3. Tsuzuki as a pioneer in *Tokyo Style*

Before *Tokyo Style*, no book had ever shown so many ordinary, small, cluttered rooms in a single anthology. Although in many ways banal, Tsuzuki's project was the first of its kind. As he explains:

> I believe in the power of *quantity*. It would not have great impact if I only took the photographs of five or ten rooms. But if I do a hundred, I should be able to build a picture of a certain world. *Quantity* is a clear expression of a person's curiosity. Although each photograph was imperfect, I believed that I could overwhelm the viewers with the energy and *quantity*.[44]

Tsuzuki's comment about quantity's ability to build a picture of a world has precedent in the history of photography. August Sander's *People of the 20th Century* (1876-1964) is a highly influential work in both photography and fashion that set out to capture and group portraits of hundreds of people according to various so-

---

[43] Toki, pp.124-125.

[44] Toki, p.127.

cial strata.[45] According to Susanne Lange, when Sander exhibited some 600 of his photographs in Cologne in 1927 (divided into seven groups - 'The Farmer', 'The Skilled Tradesman', 'Classes and Professionals', 'The Woman', 'The Artists', 'The City' and 'The Last People'), it amounted 'to a visual record of the different types, occupations, social classes and family structures of his era… the work as a whole could be regarded as a universal picture of society, a model that, in terms of both its methods and contents, reaches far beyond the original context of its making'.[46] The sheer volume of photographs that Sander presented generated impact, forming a view of a world previously undocumented. Tsuzuki's work follows something akin to this method of photographic documentation, although Sander is unlikely to have been a direct influence on him.

4. Tsuzki's influence on young Japanese people

Tokyo Style inspired a number of young Japanese people living in similar apartments to those depicted in the book. Tsuzuki notes:

> I received a lot of letters from the readers. Most of them said that they were inspired by the book. They had often read magazines or watched TV that had shown luxurious interiors and had become depressed by the comparison with their own living conditions, which were not as

---

[45] Wim Wenders, *Yohji Yamamoto by Wim Wenders*, (London: BBC2, 1991). In this film Yamamoto states that he has been inspired by the uniforms and garments of people in Sander's *People of the 20th Century*.

[46] Susanne Lange, 'August Sander's People of the 20th Century: Its Making and Impact' in *Cruel and Tender*, (London: Tate, 2003), p.29.

beautiful or richly decorated. But they realised that there were worse rooms than their own apartments![47]

Few young Japanese people are confident about their living conditions. Apartments, especially in Tokyo, tend to be small (a 15sqm studio flat is not atypical) and so people rarely invite friends to their apartments – they simply don't have the space. This contrasts with young people living in London, for example, who may share a house with communal spaces. Even if their own room is small, there are areas in the remainder of the house where they can entertain.

Happy Victims is a great source for ethnographic study of fashion and the phenomenon of privacy in contemporary urban spaces. Tsuzuki says:

> Basing the approach on *Tokyo Style*, I wanted to investigate the type of person who is homosexual, for example, living alone in the centre of Tokyo, and is obsessed with one single fashion brand such as Comme des Garçons. I wanted to find out what the person does for a living and what kind of accommodation the person lives in.[48]

HAPPY VICTIMS: KYOICHI TSUZUKI'S PHOTOGRAPHIC SERIES IN *RYUKO TSUSHIN* MAGAZINE

1. The description of *Happy Victims*

Happy Victims was incorporated into *Ryuko Tsushin*, a magazine dominated by highly stylised fashion photography. This setting

---

[47] Toki, pp.130-131.

[48] Tsuzuki, personal interview.

contrasted with the realism of the *Happy Victims* series, thereby creating a greater impact on readers. Figure 3 is taken from *Happy Victims* and is a good example of the type of photograph typically featured in the series.

On the right-hand side of Figure 3 are accompanying texts that describe the woman's house, her family background, and how Gianfranco Ferre came into her life:

> A house in suburban Chiba, about an hour east of central Tokyo. Here in this perfectly normal dwelling lives a perfectly normal family of four. One of the two daughters, however, just happens to be a top-class Gianfranco Ferre collector. With 'no idea how many pieces I've got' she starts pulling out clothes and just look: Here's a 900 thousand yen dress, a 1 million yen stole (scarf) and 1.2 million yen coat! What's such super-glamourous Ferre haute couture doing in an ordinary kiddy bedroom? It's all too surreal. Here's her childhood study desk perfectly mismatched with a cocktail party evening dress, yet rather than clash they create a mysterious kind of parallel reality. Her fascination with the exclusive brand Ferre began while still in school when she saw his beautiful designs in the *25 ans* magazine. After graduation she found work in an apparel company, and it's been a 15-year love affair ever since. 'Ferre's appeal is the gorgeous sense of fulfilment you get wearing him'. She explains simply. But wait, 'I can't wear him when I am not feeling well'. Meaning, she needs to be in the right mood to brave wearing such extravagance. How true. Just for the record, her parents are also in the clothing business: her mother is an ex-designer and her father a long-time veteran of the garment trade. 'There are lots of suits and ties buried in my closet I have only worn maybe twice', the father says. Is the fashion addiction hereditary!?[49]

A summation of the woman's daily routine follows the texts:

---

[49] Kyoichi Tsuzuki, *Happy Victims*, Volume 56, in *Ryuko Tsushin*, translated by Alfred Birnbaum, (Tokyo: INFAS Publications, 2003). p.148.

Figure 3: *Happy Victims*, Volume 56 in *Ryuko Tsushin*, December 2003. This woman's room is filled with fashion pieces by Gianfranco Ferre.

08:00 Get up
08:30 Leave the house
09:50 Start work
14:00 Go to convenience store, buy lunch
21:00 Leave the office
22:00 Get home, eat dinner
03:00 Turn in

  Throughout the series, the texts about the inhabitants' lives are consistently followed by a breakdown of their daily schedule. In the photographs, most of the inhabitants' faces are blurred, or else they are depicted lying down on the sofa or bed to hide their face. Paradoxically, while they are happy to reveal the identities they have constructed through their clothes and personal space, they don't want to show their faces. This aspect of Tsuzuki's photographs adds an air of mystery to his subjects. Why show off, but not show yourself?

Writing in *Image Music Text*, Roland Barthes states that 'the photograph allows the photographer to conceal elusively the preparation to which he subjects the scene to be recorded'.[50] Barthes argues that a photograph carries 'connotations', which give 'the impression of second meaning on the photographic message'.[51] This second meaning is built from 'the scene itself, the literal reality'[52] through different processes, such as choice of subjects, technical treatment (for example, lighting, exposure and printing), framing, texts and lay-out. Together, these form the second meaning (which is the result of the actions of the creator)[53] of the photograph as a whole.[54] In the case of Figure 3, 'the scene itself, the literal reality' are the woman, her clothes, shoes, the lampshade and the air conditioner in her room, while the 'result of the action of the creator' is what Tsuzuki and *Ryuko Tsushin* have co-created – the choice of subject, camera, lighting, exposure, texts, layout and printing. *Happy Victims* is a fine example of Barthes's theory in action.

Barthes's structural analysis of how techniques contribute to the second meaning of a photograph is broken down into the fol-

---

[50] Roland Barthes, *Image Music Text*, translated by Stephen Heath, (London: Fontana Paperbacks, 1977), p.21.

[51] Barthes, p.20.

[52] Barthes, p.17.

[53] Barthes, p.17.

[54] Barthes, p.20.

lowing categories: 'Trick effects', 'Pose', 'Objects', 'Photographia', 'Aestheticism', and 'Syntax'. The 'Photographia' category provides a useful interpretation of the blurring in Tsuzuki's photographs:

> In photographia the connoted message is the image itself, 'embellished' (which is to say in general sublimated) by techniques of lighting, exposure and printing. An inventory needs to be made of these techniques, but only insofar as each of them has a corresponding signified of connotation sufficiently constant to allow its incorporation in a cultural lexicon of technical 'effects' (as for instance the 'blurring of movement'...)[55]

Photographs represent images transferred from subjects in front of the lens, 'embellished' by effects such as lighting, camera type, the specific photographer, and the subject's movement. The meaning of the photograph therefore results from the photographer's vision to transform the input of these different elements into an integrated whole – a process which creates a style and aesthetic unique to the photographer. In Tsuzuki's photographs, the movement of the inhabitant's head (the photograph is taken on a long exposure) results in the blurring of the face of the subject. Tsuzuki's own input and influence on how the photograph has been taken is, as Barthes says, 'concealed elusively' in his photographic series.

2. Readership of *Ryuko Tsushin*

Launched in 1966, *Ryuko Tsushin* was a women's magazine that reported on high-fashion trends from major capitals such as Lon-

---

[55] Barthes, p.23.

don, Paris, Milan, New York and Tokyo. It included photography stories based on seasonal themes; sections on specific high-fashion brands; reports on fashion shows from around the world; and interviews with fashion designers, artists, actors, supermodels and other such figures. The basic style of *Ryuko Tsushin* was similar to *Vogue*, but it seemed more niche, less commercial, and was targeted at a smaller group of people who were interested in high-fashion as well as music, movies and culture (areas in which the magazine did not always feature mainstream works). The circulation of the magazine was not as large as *Vogue* – after its relaunch in August 2006 it claimed to have a circulation of 150,000. Pre-relaunch, about 90 per cent of the magazine's readers were female; 60 per cent were in their twenties and 19 per cent in their thirties. In terms of its readers' occupations, 44 per cent were students, and 18 per cent were freelancers such as photographers, stylists and designers.[56]

3. Tsuzuki's photographic style in *Happy Victims*

In some respects, Tsuzuki's photographic style is fundamentally new – while his images take established aspects of fashion, documentary and fine art photography, they blur these elements to new effect. Although Tsuzuki worked for *Ryuko Tsushin* on a commercial basis, his photography cannot easily be categorised as fashion photography and the series undoubtedly incorporates elements of fine art. Ulrich Lehmann suggests that 'fashion photography has to manoeuvre between the twin poles of commercial viability and

---

[56] *Ryuko Tsushin* press kit, (Tokyo: INFAS Publications, 2006)

creative expression',[57] further analysing the different aspects that fashion photography possesses: the photographer, the model, gestures, the narrative, and text. Some of these aspects fit Tsuzuki's photography, but not all of them. Lehmann argues, for instance, that fashion photographers take 'the material expression of the human body through clothing',[58] going on to say that fashion photography possesses an 'accepted material and aesthetic system: you have to be properly dressed and not appear old-fashioned'.[59] This is where Tsuzuki's style starts to differ from the accepted norm: many of the subjects in his photographs are dressed in clothing that are not the latest releases – after all, they are part of archives which may stretch back many years, rather than being the latest releases. Lehmann defines the latest fashions as those that are worn by models in highly stylised and constructed settings; Tsuzuki's photographs depict real people in their actual homes with their favourite possessions, accumulated over time. In this sense, *Happy Victims* does not fit the genre of fashion photography.

    Lehmann notes that 'one of the most distinctive features of fashion photography is the narrative'.[60] In fashion photography, this narrative is usually a short amount of text setting the scene for the photoshoot – perhaps describing the shoot's location or its storyboard background. There is narrative in Tsuzuki's photographs, but not in the strict definition of fashion photography nar-

---

[57] Ulrich Lehmann, *Chic Clicks*, (New York: Hatje Cantz Publishers, 2002), p.T4.

[58] Lehmann, p.T4.

[59] Lehmann, p.T7.

[60] Lehmann, p.T10.

rative provided by Lehmann. In the context of fashion magazines in general, Lehmann goes on to say that 'the editorial in particular is fashion's characteristic device to invest and construct a story around clothing. This story can have a conventional, linear syntax or it can consist of repeated variations on a theme'.[61] The motivation for accompanying photographs with a story is usually commercial: to encourage readers to consume the fashion featured in the photographs. The narrative in Tsuzuki's *Happy Victims*, by contrast, is not there to promote the latest designs – instead, it is a biography of the subject in relation to their chosen brand.

The subjects in Tsuzuki's photographs are not necessarily wealthy, they have simply chosen to devote the bulk of their income to a particular fashion brand. *Ryuko Tsushin* was premised on featuring traditional high-fashion photographs that create 'fantasies'[62] alongside more realistic reports on new concept stores and sections exploring the latest trends. This is what Jennifer Craik calls 'explicitness in technique' and it can be applied to *Ryuko Tsushin's* editorial fashion shoots.[63] Craik argues:

> Decisive moments and turning points in fashion photography have been celebrated as capturing the spirit of an era… Fashion photography has constituted both techniques of representation and techniques of self-formation. It has served as an index of changing ideas about fashion and gender, and about body-habits relations. As well as constituting a record of fashion moments, fashion photography has become the main

---

[61] Lehmann, p.T10.

[62] Jeniffer Craik, *The Face of Fashion*, (London: Routledge, 1993), p.92.

[63] Craik, p.92.

source of knowledge about clothes and bodies in a practical way and in processes of historical accounting.[64]

Craik's comments reflect high-fashion photography in general, which depicts models dressed in high-fashion items and further embellished with hair, make-up and accessories (for an example, see Figure 4). As Craik argues, these photographs project 'the spirit of an era', but they do not depict real consumers. Instead, their subjects are professional models shot in a studio setting with strobe flash lighting. Although these photographs do '[serve] as an index of changing ideas about fashion and gender, and about body-habits relations' with the combination of 'techniques of representation' and 'techniques of self-formation', they are not based on the lives of ordinary people. Lehmann's interpretation of fashion photography is similar:

> Fashion photography, in following the suggestions of the fashion industry about the latest figure, measurements and proportions, declares a new beauty each season: a beauty that is fugitive, ephemeral and insubstantial, yet exerts a powerful hold on corporeal ideals, often perceived by the spectator only through the mediating and distorting eye of the camera.[65]

In this context, stylists call in samples of the latest fashions, creating 'the looks of the season' prior to the photo shoot and then dressing models with them on set. Hair stylists and make-up artists then elaborate the models' faces to further suggest the 'new beauty' of each season. The models are given directions about how to pro-

---

[64] Craik, pp.92-93.

[65] Lehmann, p.T9.

Figure 4: *Ryuko Tsushin*, Volume 486, December 2003, photographed by Kazunali Tajima.

ject the narrative to the camera, creating an artificially constructed image – what Craik means by fashion photography constituting 'techniques of self-formation'. This notion can be seen in the idealised representations of clothes on beautiful models, artificially constructed through the 'mediating and distorting eye of the camera'. These idealised scenarios deliberately strive to engender an aspiration in the reader to replicate the 'corporeal ideals' represented within fashion photography.

John Clammer is also useful for interpreting Craik's ideas of 'techniques of representation' and 'techniques of self-formation'. Clammer discusses the representation of fashion in media as such: 'Essentially the social construction of body can be regarded as product commercialisation..., it is a presentation to adapt the images that demonstrate "body should look like this" being led by media'.[66] Clammer also argues that the construction of images is a standard human activity connected to market forces: products are continually consumed and, to enable new consumer demand, images continually change to reflect new fashions.[67]

Craik also explains that '[fashion] photographs are quite conspicuous constructions, portraying an unreal, glamorous world designed to seduce and to captivate the viewer'.[68] High-fashion photographs are essentially 'conspicuous', 'unreal' and project 'fantasy' in fashion magazines. Tsuzuki's work has a different purpose from fashion photography.

4. Yutaka Ishibashi: Social caste depicted in *Happy Victims*

Tsuzuki photographed about 90 people to 'display the relationships between clothes, wearers and contexts'.[69] Generally, the subjects of *Happy Victims* are a particular type of fashion consumer. Usually aged in their early twenties to late thirties, and living in Tokyo (or just outside of the city), they have a wide range of occupations. Some work in the creative industries, such as fashion, design and architecture, while others are sales assistants, teachers, and salarymen. Volume 47, for example, highlights a salaryman who works

---

[66] John Clammer, *Contemporary Urban Japan*, translated by Kazutaka Hashimoto, Izumi Hotta, Hidehiro Takahashi and Hiroko Yoshimoto, (Kyoto: Minerva Publications, 2001), p.181.

[67] Clammer, p.181.

[68] Craik, p.101.

[69] Craik, p.93.

for an advertising company (Figure 5). This man loves Thierry Mugler and his obsession with the brand stems from his occupation, as the accompanying text makes clear: 'when he first started working, his boss told him the salaryman's suit is his battle wear'.[70] When the man first went to a department store in search of appropriate work attire, he came across Thierry Mugler and has continued to buy the same brand ever since.[71]

Yutaka Ishibashi, the subject of Volume 48, was similarly obsessed, albeit with a different fashion brand – Maison Martin Margiela ⑩ (Figure 6). Ishibashi was a typical example of a young Japanese consumer obsessed with high-fashion items, investing large amounts of time and money in a single brand. What singles him out as a particularly extreme example of a Happy Victim, however, is the meticulous care he takes with his clothes and accessories, and the way he operates in his living space in order to preserve his items.

Ishibashi was an instructor at the Bunka Fashion College, a prestigious fashion college from which Kenzo Takada, Yohji Yamamoto and Jun Takahashi of Undercover all graduated. He has been obsessed with Martin Margiela's collections for over a decade, deriving considerable pleasure from being surrounded by the designer's clothes and accessories at his home. Ishibashi's students even called him 'Maestro Margiela' because of his obsessive atti-

---

[70] Kyoichi Tsuzuki, *Happy Victims*, Volume 47, *Ryuko Tsushin*, (Tokyo: INFAS Publications, March 2003), p.142.

[71] Tsuzuki, p.142.

Figure 5: *Happy Victims*, Volume 47, in *Ryuko Tsushin*, March 2003.

tude, as mentioned in the accompanying text shown in Figure 6.[72] Ishibashi's obsession has become so notorious that it has now extended to recognition from the public as a result of the article. It is very rare for a consumer to become famous for their obsession with a single brand.

Ishibashi's behaviour is representative of the type of person who purchases fashion products from just one designer. As soon as he was paid each month, Ishibashi spent all of his available salary on Margiela's designs. According to his accompanying text in Volume 48, Ishibashi invests about 2m yen on Margiela products every season.[73] Not only does he purchase a huge number of

---

[72] Kyoichi Tsuzuki, *Happy Victims*, Volume 48, *Ryuko Tsushin*, (Tokyo: INFAS Publications, April 2003), pp.150-151.

[73] Tsuzuki, p.150.

clothes and accessories, but he is also highly scrupulous about preserving his items. In the accompanying text, Tsuzuki describes Ishibashi's meticulousness:

> No normal obsession, he stretches forward when eating so as not to dirty his precious clothes… No drying outside either, because smog will stick to the clothes; he uses a hanger rack to dry everything indoors, each item in a specific order. He'd rather eat out than infuse his clothes with daily life smells, and only keeps eye drops in the refrigerator. He's never once lit the stove or run the water in the kitchen, keeping only a precision stack of room-temperature processed soy milk packs. No wastebasket even. When he gets thirsty, he rushes to the nearby shop and drinks on the spot, taking the trash out at the same time to discard at the store. No men are allowed to piss in the john standing up, lest they cause a mess. This is a man after Margiela's heart (not to mention his landlord's).[74]

Margiela graduated from the Royal Academy of Fine Arts of Antwerp in 1979, working as a design assistant for Jean Paul Gaultier until 1987 when he established Maison Martin Margiela in Paris, creating his first womenswear collection in 1988.[75] Margiela's conceptual products attracted core fashion fans and industry figures. His shop interiors were painted white, with no obvious external sign. Margiela himself has never appeared in the media, nor issued a press release. As a result of this silence, the philosophy and concept behind his collections have been the subject of serious debate by fashion journalists and scholars. Christopher Breward's book *Fashion* addresses Margiela's theoretical presentation by stating 'Margiela's most notable pieces appear to challenge traditional

---

[74] Tsuzuki, p.150.

[75] Index of Maison Martin Margiela, *http://www.martinmargiela.com*.

Figure 6: *Happy Victims*, Volume 48, in *Ryuko Tsushin*, April 2003.

means of constructing and contextualising clothing, subjecting the structure and life of a garment to an intense scrutiny that is more usually found in academic rather than commercial fora'.[76] Indeed, Margiela's products do not overtly express a brand identity in the fashion of Dolce and Gabbana, for instance. Instead, Margiela's branding is restricted to four stitches subtly positioned on the nape of the garment. None of the pieces carry a logo per se.

According to the PR director of Maison Martin Margiela ⑩, Margiela decided not to appear in public or comment in the media as Gaultier does because he questioned whether a designer should form a part of the promotion of their product. Margiela saw how Gaultier often accepted media interviews, subsequently becoming

---

[76] Christopher Breward, *Fashion*, (Oxford: Oxford University Press, 2003), pp.237-238.

a fashion icon and an integral part of the brand. Margiela wanted to do the opposite: he expected consumers to focus purely on the designer's products, not the designer's personality as represented in the media. Margiela wished to avoid using himself as a promotional tool for his own business.[77]

In an interview I conducted with Ishibashi in the summer of 2006, other aspects of his obsession with Margiela, not featured in the *Happy Victims* article, came to light.[78] The purpose of the interview was to find out more about his life with his collection, and understand what had changed in his life, philosophy and room since the photographs were published three years earlier.

Ishibashi said: 'I always take care of the position of the rails in my room so as not to expose them to the daylight (Figure 7). And I do not keep things on the floor, because the dust is supposed to stick to things and my room would be filthy. It is bad for my clothes.'[79] Ishibashi organises his clothes on hanging rails and plans his weekly outfits in advance: 'I preserve my clothes only by hanging them. No items such as trousers or knitwear are folded up, otherwise I cannot see all my items and organise a whole week's plan of outfits. Actually, my entire outfit plan is based on a two or three week rotation, which is always in my head. Once I wear a

---

[77] PR director of Maison Martin Margiela ⑩, personal conversation, (Paris, 28 January 2007). Due to the company's philosophy, the individual's name cannot be disclosed.

[78] Yutaka Ishibashi, personal interview, (Tokyo, 19 September 2006).

[79] Ishibashi, personal interview.

Figure 7: The rails reserved for Margiela tops in Ishibashi's room.

specific item I would not wear it within the following two weeks.'[80]

Ishibashi has stopped wearing aftershave, as it includes artificial colours which could stain his clothes. Instead he burns Patchouli, an aromatic oil that is burned in all Margiela's shops (Figure 8), so that he can replicate the scent of the shop not only in his room, but also on his clothes which absorb the fragrance. Ishibashi feels happy about being surrounded by his Margiela collection: simply looking at the clothes satisfies him.[81] His life is entirely dedicated to the products of Martin Margiela and, although he has been living in the same small apartment for many years, he

---

[80] Ishibashi.

[81] Ishibashi.

is completely content with his living arrangements and life choices – a Happy Victim of Martin Margiela, as the series title indicates. As Ishibashi related his lifestyle to me during the interview, he admitted that he had the instincts of a collector. Is he a fashion Otaku? Ishibashi made clear to me that he did not wish to be categorised as such.

The case study of Ishibashi illustrates the connection between the subjects of the *Happy Victims* series and Otaku. In the next chapter, Okaku culture in Japan will be examined and I will highlight the common threads that connect people such as Ishibashi with Otaku.

Figure 8: Patchouli diffuser in Ishibashi's room. All the garments are by Martin Margiela.

Chapter Two
Otaku -
from minority to majority as participatory consumers

WHO IS OTAKU?

Is it possible to define the Happy Victims as fashion Otaku or fashion victims? 'Otaku', after all, is a word that typically 'evokes a stereotyped image of an unfashionable computer nerd, preoccupied with games and Anime (animations) even after his adolescence'.[82] This chapter discusses the emergence of Otaku culture in the 1980s and how these people relate to the Happy Victims.

Otaku culture first emerged in the mid-1980s in Akihabara, one of the central districts of Tokyo where there is an unrivalled concentration of electronics stores. Many Otaku visit this area because of these stores' specialisation in personal computers. Today, Akihabara has become one of Tokyo's most popular tourist centres because of its extreme concentration of computers, household gadgets and other products.[83]

To analyse this in more depth, the book *The Research on the Otaku Market* by the Nomura Research Institute should be introduced. The basic definitions of the term Otaku that this publication proposes are:

1. Those who develop a particular and strong interest in a certain category of consumer goods
2. They concentrate their time and money exclusively on the category

---

[82] Kenzo Tange, Toshio Okada, Yoshiaki Kaihatsu, Yuki Oshima and Tamaki Sato, 'OTAKU: personality = space = cities', Japanese Pavilion at the 9th Biennale International Architecture Exhibition in 2004 (accessed on 1 February 2007).

[83] Kenzo Tange, Toshio Okada, Yoshiaki Kaihatsu, Yuki Oshima and Tamaki Sato, 'OTAKU: personality = space = cities'.

Figure 9: An image of Otaku, displayed in the Japanese Pavilion at the 9th Biennale International Architecture Exhibition.

3. They have profound knowledge of the particular category of consumer goods, in which they often develop creatively and share with others.[84]

In the early 1980s, 'Otaku' took on negative connotations as a result of the Miyazaki murders, something I described in the introduction to this book. This was not only because Otaku were so particular about their chosen interests, but also because of how they communicated through internet chat rooms and Comic Market, which will be discussed later in the chapter. Otaku culture became visible in society in the late 1980s, and the majority of people perceived it as nerdy, anti-social and, as a result of the murders,

---

[84] Nomura Research Institute, *The Research on the Otaku Market*, (Tokyo: Toyo Keizai Inc., 2005), p.2.

potentially even dangerous. During the 1990s, however, the Otaku had transformed this negative meaning, adopting the term as if sneering at themselves – a form of irony and reclamation. Among young Japanese people, 'Otaku' – and related terms such as 'mania' and 'collector' – became popular in this period.[85]

Otaku people are participatory consumers who invest in products such as animation, video games and computers. By self-investment, they develop their knowledge and ideas in the field, and even create new products based on the originals that they purchase. John Fiske's argument in his article 'The Cultural Economy of Fandom' is useful here:

> 'Investing' in education, in acquiring certain cultural tastes and competences, will produce a social 'return' in terms of better job prospects, of enhanced social prestige and thus of a higher socio-economic position. Cultural capital thus works hand in hand with economic capital to produce social privilege and distinction.[86]

This is Fiske's interpretation of Pierre Bourdieu's argument in *Distinction*, which describes 'culture as an economy in which people invest and accumulate capital'.[87] Fiske goes on to say that the cultural system works unequally and therefore distinguishes between 'the privileged' and 'the developed'. This system legitimises a particular 'high' culture through its educational system and institutions such as art galleries and museums. Participation in

---

[85] Nomura Research Institute, p.2.

[86] John Fiske, 'The Cultural Economy of Fandom' in *The Adoring Audience: Fan Culture and Popular Media*, edited by Lisa A. Lewis (London: Routledge, 1992), p.31.

[87] Fiske, pp.30-31.

this 'official' culture requires considerable money. Higher education is expensive, yet a degree is normally deemed essential if you are to specialise in a particular field of art (or fashion). The system therefore distinguishes between people who possess 'a higher socio-economic position' and those who do not. In the first two decades of the 21st century, I noticed a number of wealthy Chinese students attending institutions such as Central Saint Martins, MIT and NYU: during the years of the bubble economy, this same observation might have been made of Japanese students. These demographics reflect the economic realities of each country at particular moments in their history. Unfortunately, it would be rare for someone from a poor family to be able to afford such an education. This exclusivity, however, is opposed to sub-culture, which is not yet mainstream and therefore has no institutional support by way of legitimisation.[88]

By self-investing, Otaku educate themselves and acquire knowledge or 'cultural taste', although this culture is not perceived as 'legitimate' by the majority of people who appreciate 'high' culture. By accumulating knowledge, Otaku become producers or taste makers in their particular category, based on their experience in accordance with their investment of time and money. Some of them may acquire a 'higher socio-economic position'– becoming specialists through their knowledge and creativity in a field – thus contributing to the construction of a new culture, and creating new consumption or new 'fans'. This is how Otaku have acquired social 'distinction' in Japan during the 1990s, becoming recognised as contributors to its culture and economy.

---

[88] Fiske, p.31.

Figure 10: Paper craft figures made by Otaku.

OTAKU AS PART OF THE JAPANESE MAINSTREAM SINCE THE 1990s; ANALYSIS OF COMIC MARKET

Today, Otaku culture is part of mainstream Japanese society, not only because of its popularity, but also because of the size of Otaku business. The economic contribution by Otaku is enormous, and the business built off the back of Otaku culture is accordingly huge. I will demonstrate this based on my field research at Comic Market in December 2006, relating this to Fiske's argument on fan culture.

Fiske argues that 'Fans, in particular, are active producers and users of such cultural capital and, at the level of fan organiza-

Figure 11: A company's stand with campaign girls and Otaku photographing them.

tion, begin to produce equivalents of the formal institutions of official culture'.[89] This is explicit in Japanese Otaku culture, although it is now becoming an 'official' culture, rather than remaining the underground or unofficial phenomenon it has been in the past. Comic Market is a biannual event, each edition of which runs for three days in Tokyo. It is extremely popular. According to the event's website, in 2006 the event attracted around 130,000 visitors on its first day, 150,000 on its second, and 160,000 on its final day.[90] It has continued to grow. In December 2019, Comic Market was a four-day event and visited by around 750,000 people – the

---

[89] Fiske, p.33.

[90] The Official Comic Market website, *http://www.comiket.co.jp/info-a/C71/C71AfterRepost.html,* (accessed on 1 February 2007).

highest number since the event started in 1975 in a small meeting room.[91] It is hosted in the Tokyo Big Sight, a gigantic venue in the bayside area which has two main entrances – the East and West gates. The East gate holds individual stands that sell, amongst other things, original comics, cartoons and action figures (at the time of my visit, these were 'unofficial', see Figure 10), whereas the West gate hosts a number of company stands such as Toshiba Entertainment that welcome Otaku people with 'campaign girls' (see Figure 11) and sell new products such as posters and DVDs (these are, obviously, 'official'). The East gate is where individual Otaku display their creativity based on their investigation and experiences of watching animation or cartoons, sharing their knowledge with visitors. In the West gate, animation or cartoon companies promote their new products and services.

Individual Otaku and companies are clearly segregated in the East and West gate respectively. Otaku organise themselves into circles with other Otaku who share their interests, producing 'equivalent objects' or 'remixed products' to the 'official' culture of the companies. However, as the number of participants increases and their creativity develops, the creations of individual Otaku are becoming ever more popular. One consequence of this trend is that Otaku are now becoming the producers of an 'official' culture. While their consumption used to be marginal, it is now entering the mainstream market.

This phenomenon means that 'Otaku' is now used casually in order to describe any number of people: fashion Otaku; Kenko or health Otaku (those obsessed with healthy diets, ingredients, yoga,

---

[91] Kai You, *https://kai-you.net/article/70630,* (accessed on 5 September 2020).

and so forth); Ongaku or music Otaku (the three definitions of Otaku by the Nomura Research Institute remind me of professional DJs – their enormous record collections are their knowledge, and also become their creativity); Eiga or film Otaku (the director Quentin Tarantino is a great example), and so on. These expressions are used as a compliment to admire a person's speciality, experience and knowledge, although still imply that Otaku are a bit insular (although perhaps not entirely, as these people still enjoy going to events, as I described earlier). Some Otaku have even acquired a certain 'distinction' as a result of their outstanding experience, knowledge and skills. In this way, the connotations of the term have changed from purely negative to mainly positive.

This transition can be partly explained by looking at the trajectory of Japanese consumption since the early 1980s. Over this period, consumption of imported goods has flourished thanks to the strength of the yen (see Introduction for more details). People have had more disposable income to afford products such as comics, records, clothes, cars and organic foodstuffs. Especially in fashion, imported luxury products from Europe have become far more accessible. With this growth in consumption, there has been a growth in cultural wealth too.

At the same time as these developments, Japanese animation, comics and fashion were becoming highly valued internationally. Due to this international recognition, Otaku became aware of their uniqueness in their chosen fields. In the UK, for instance, BBC3 aired the TV show *Japanorama*, presented by Jonathan Ross, in 2002. This show reported on areas of Japanese contemporary culture, including Otaku, and the show became popular.[92] Takuro Morinaga, an economist who worked at Mitsubishi UFJ Research & Consulting until 2007, describes a shopping arcade in Beijing as being 'just like Akihabara' – there were around 100 shops that sell Otaku-related products. In South Korea, Japanese animations have become popular, and programmes broadcasted in Japan can be watched online just 30 minutes after their terrestrial broadcast.[93] Internationally, Otaku have become accepted as producers of Japanese culture – a remarkable turnaround from when they were a minority group only decades earlier.[94]

FAN CULTURE - A PSYCHOLOGICAL APPROACH

As previously explained, John Fiske's argument is useful for analysis of Otaku culture, which has a connection with 'fan culture'. According to Fiske, fan culture forms a 'shadow cultural economy' that 'lies outside of the cultural industries yet shares features with them which more normal popular culture lacks'.[95] 'Fandom' is often outside or against official culture on the one hand, but on the other, 'it expropriates and reworks certain values and characteristics of that official culture to which it is opposed',[96]

---

[92] *Brutus*, (Tokyo: Magazine House, January 2007), p.35.

[93] Takuro Morinaga, *Moe Economics*, (Tokyo: Kodansha, 2005), pp.15-24.

[94] Nomura Research Institute, p.4.

[95] Fiske, p.30.

[96] Fiske, p.34.

thereby acquiring a certain position in society. With regard to this, Fiske states:

> Fans discriminate fiercely... the boundaries between the community of fans and the rest of the world are just as strongly marked and patrolled. Both sides of boundary invest in the difference; mundane viewers often wish to avoid what they see as the taint of fandom.[97]

Ishibashi, for instance, is obsessed with buying Margiela's products, fashions himself by wearing those garments every day, and through these habits has acquired deep knowledge about Margiela's creations. But Ishibashi does not want to be recognised as a fashion Otaku.

One possible reason for this is that Ishibashi wishes to avoid what 'mundane viewers' see as 'the taint of fandom' and tries to include himself in the rest of society, rather than in what is perceived as an extreme community. Ishibashi may have a strong sense of 'the boundaries between the community of fans and the rest of the world', and he simultaneously wishes to use the boundaries to be free from the 'taint of fandom'. My case study focuses on an unordinary consumer, as this is what *Happy Victims* is all about.

This boundary between 'normal' and 'abnormal' is usefully elaborated by Joli Jenson in her psychoanalytic text 'Fandom as Pathology: The Consequences of Characterization'. Jenson demonstrates that 'the fan is consistently characterized as a potential fa-

---

[97] Fiske, p.34-35.

natic',[98] and that fandom is described by images of deviance. There is an ambiguous borderline between 'normal' and excessive fandom which can be crossed when reality and fantasy are blurred. Imagine falling in love with a celebrity though the media (virtual), and being so lovestruck that you cannot fall asleep for thinking about them (real) – in such a case, reality and fantasy have blurred. It is interesting to observe Jenson's description of how people may distance themselves from those they perceive as fanatic fans:

> Fandom, is what 'they' do; 'we' on the other hand, have tastes and preferences, and select worthy people, beliefs and activities for our admiration and esteem. Furthermore, what 'they' do is deviant, and therefore dangerous, while what 'we' do is normal, therefore safe.[99]

Jenson believes that there are two crucial aspects for this cognitive process – 'the objects of desire' and 'the modes of enactment'. The objects of desire are usually deemed as high culture – 'paintings not posters, the *New York Review of Books* not the *National Enquirer*'. If the object of desire is popular with the lower or middle classes (that is, it is inexpensive and widely available), it is fandom. 'The modes of enactment' are a valuation of the genteel over the rowdy, based in class and social distinctions.[100] If it is popular with the wealthy and well educated (this implies expensive

---

[98] Joli Jenson, 'Fandom as Pathology: The Consequences of Characterization' in *The Adoring Audience: Fan Culture and Popular Media*, edited by Lisa A. Lewis (London: Routledge, 1992), p.9.

[99] Jenson, p.19.

[100] Jenson, p.20.

and rare), it is preference, interest or expertise.[101] A good example of this in action are the (generally) respectful fans at Wimbledon tennis matches, as opposed to crowds at football matches. Applause at Wimbledon should be kept short, and the crowd may be warned if the umpire deems them rowdy, whereas thunderous shouting and chanting is expected at football stadiums. Wimbledon happens once a year (rarity) and tickets are more expensive than those for football, which takes place over the course of the year. A tennis fan might say: 'Do "we" riot outside the stadium? Never! Football fans – "they" do!'

Ishibashi said that he does not want to be recognised as Otaku and has possibly retained the term's stereotype of animation, manga and computer nerds. Ishibashi may think about Otaku in the same way as Jenson describes, that what 'they' do is deviant and 'dangerous', while what 'he' does is normal and therefore 'safe'. In addition, Ishibashi can recognise his activity as 'high culture'. Margiela's products are not as widely available as animation, manga or computer games, and they are expensive. Thus his 'objects of desire' and 'modes of enactment' could be categorised as 'expertise'.

After Ishibashi's life was featured in *Ryuko Tsushin*, Margiela came across the article and republished Tsuzuki's photograph in his own publication, *A magazine*. No matter how Ishibashi perceives himself, to readers of *Ryuko Tsushin* and, seemingly, Margiela himself, he looks obsessive. This may be a psychological paradox of Otaku – on the one hand, the individual is dominated by a certain product or culture (partly via the media) which may

---

[101] Jenson, p.19.

blur their reality and fantasy, on the other hand, they are still involved in 'normal' society and may perceive what 'others' do as deviant or abnormal. In Japan, the stereotype of Otaku was heavily influenced by the Miyazaki murders, resulting in a situation in which being identified as Otaku carried a stigma. To alleviate this, many Otaku conceived of themselves as operating in 'normal' society, categorising others as 'different from us'.

Fiske also introduces the idea of 'enunciative productivity'[102], which is a public mechanism through which fans can share knowledge within a face-to-face or oral culture. Comic Market is a great example, as is the way in which colleagues or friends may constantly talk about a particular band, sport team or TV show, allowing others to be drawn into their fandom as a means of joining that particular social group. Fiske picks up the example of Madonna fans:

> But important though talk is, it is not the only means of enunciation available. The styling of hair or make-up, the choice of clothes or accessories are ways of constructing a social identity and therefore of asserting one's membership of a particular fan community. The Madonna fans who, on MTV, claimed that dressing like Madonna made people take more notice of them as they walked down the street were not only constructing for themselves more empowered identities than those normally available to young adolescent girls but were putting those meanings into social circulation.[103]

---

[102] Fiske, p.37.

[103] Fiske, p.38.

This is a form of semiotic productivity that is 'characteristic of popular culture'.[104] 'The fans "became" Madonna in a way that denied any distance between performer and audience; they participated in constructing and circulating the "meanings of Madonnaness" in their own culture'.[105] In Ishibashi's case, by wearing Margiela's clothes from head to toe, he perhaps 'becomes' Margiela and projects the 'meanings of Margielaness'. If so, how does the rest of society react to this participatory attitude towards Margielaness?

When I spoke to him, Ishibashi explained why he decided not to have his face blurred in Tsuzuki's image of him and his collection (Figure 6) – a choice that contrasted with many of the other Happy Victims, some of whom were unsure about being featured in a magazine. 'I just wanted to show how fantastic Margiela's creativity is,' he said. 'I recognise this as part of my activities of propagation in Japan. I think I am the missionary for Martin Margiela. Therefore it is not showing off at all to me, although some people regard this series as a stage to show off our collection'.[106] While Ishibahi is by no means an ordinary consumer, how can his attitude towards consumption be understood? What are we to make of his singular fascination with the work of one designer and his self-projection as a kind of expert? How should we frame the painstaking care with which he looks after his clothes?

Ishibashi is an undoubted expert in the work of Margiela. As Fiske argues, since Ishibashi has 'accumulated the most know-

---

[104] Fiske, p.46.

[105] Fiske, p.46.

[106] Ishibashi, personal interview.

ledge', he has been able to 'gain prestige within the group and act as opinion leader. Knowledge, like money, is always a source of power'.[107] Ishibashi should be an opinion leader around Margiela's work in the fashion industry – a person capable of making a stronger argument than others in the field. Firstly, he has gained deep knowledge about Margiela by consuming his clothes and accessories for over a decade and this is 'a source of power' for him as an instructor at the Bunka Fashion College. Secondly, he was selected as a subject of Tsuzuki's series, giving him the opportunity to be viewed by the public in an established magazine, and allowing him to become part of 'the official culture'. Thirdly, because of these first and second reasons, Ishibashi may have gained 'prestige' with fashion fans and students, enabling him to act as a 'missionary' of Margiela. Through his 'enunciative productivity', Ishibashi has managed to construct for himself a more 'empowered identity', making it possible to let his colleagues and students become drawn into a Margiela fan community at the college.

THE SIMILARITY OF OTAKU AND HAPPY VICTIMS

A few decades ago, Otaku were only able to use local networks to share their interests and relied heavily upon events to meet one another to share knowledge face to face.[108] This can also be said of people photographed for *Happy Victims* – Tsuzuki commented that many of the people he shot for the series were shy and had few friends (of course, this is not true of all of them). Even in the case

---

[107] Fiske, p.43.

[108] Nomura Research Institute, p.5.

of personal relationships, their obsessions exerted considerable influence. They may have found a particular sales assistant in their chosen fashion boutique, becoming a kind of friend to them even though they were still primarily connected to each other through a business relationship.[109] The boutique may have become a place for the Happy Victims to communicate with other people who shared their interest, and with whom they could develop their knowledge together.[110] Tsuzuki's comment could be seen as close to Jenson's observation that 'the fan (at least potentially) is an obsessed loner,[111] suffering from a disease of isolation'.

During our interview, Tsuzuki said that some of his subjects felt like they were communicating with the designers behind their favourite brands, but that this only took place in their imagined worlds. Although the Happy Victims would have been highly valued costumers, they were not invited to fashion shows, nor to exhibitions or preview parties – events at which, in theory, they should have been important guests as a result of their huge financial and cultural contribution to each brand.[112] In this context, 'cultural contribution' refers to their consumption of a brand's clothes and accessories in public, through which the Happy Victims have helped to create street culture (enunciative productivity). In Japan, well-dressed people are often photographed in the street for fashion magazines, while many international fashion designers, journalists and buyers have been inspired by Tokyo street fashion.

---

[109] Tsuzuki, personal interview.

[110] Tsuzuki, personal interview.

[111] Jenson, p.11.

[112] Tsuzuki, personal interview.

Tokyo's urban landscape is created not only by its buildings and cars, but also its obsessive consumers. Tsuzuki's 'obsessed loners' imagine that they are communicating with a designer by visiting their brand's shop and speaking with a sales assistant, as well as by consuming its products. These habits could be defined as Otaku culture.

    Most of the Happy Victims live alone in small studio flats in Tokyo. According to Jenson, 'the obsessed loner is cut off from family, friends and community. His or her life becomes increasingly dominated by an irrational fixation on a celebrity figure, a perverse attachment that dominates his or her otherwise unrewarding existence'.[113] This 'celebrity figure' could be a pop star, athlete or actor, or even a designer for fashion enthusiasts. In the world of Otaku, an anime character can be a celebrity figure too. As participants at Comic Market are captivated by animated characters, so too is Ishibashi 'dominated' by Martin Margiela as part of 'an irrational fixation on a celebrity figure'. Animation-obsessed loners, pop star-obsessed loners and fashion designer-obsessed loners are not fundamentally different, even if the media they consume is. Based on Tsuzuki's observation and Jenson's text, I would suggest that the Happy Victims can be categorised as Otaku, and that they are trying to compensate for a perceived personal lack of autonomy, absence of community, incomplete identity, and even the loneliness which they feel living in a big city like Tokyo.

---

[113] Jenson, p.15.

IS AN OTAKU A COLLECTOR?

Ishibashi has said that he may have the instincts of a collector.[114] Otaku collect their favourite consumer products, and Happy Victims collect their favourite fashion items. What are the similarities or differences between types of collector in the traditional, Western sense of the term? According to Russell W. Belk's chapter 'A Brief History of Collecting' in his book *Collecting In A Consumer Society*, after the Greek unification by the Macedonian Alexander the Great in the fourth century BCE, collecting became popular in Greece through the subsequent introduction of foreign objects and influences. Affluent Greeks collected newly imported carpets (particularly from Persia), wall hangings, furniture and paintings to display in their homes.[115] In Japan, 'royal collecting spread from China to Japan as early as the first century AD but it was not until the rise of a wealthy bourgeoisie under the Tokugawa Shogunate in the Edo era (1603-1868) that collecting spread beyond royalty, aristocrats, and the temples.'[116] Some of the collectibles were similar to the West, Belk says, 'including paintings, books, sculpture, ceramics, armour etc'[117]. Obsessive Japanese consumer behaviour may be linked with this traditional, Western notion of the collector.

Fiske says that commercial commodities are 'industrially produced and thus do not have the status of a uniquely crafted art-

---

[114] Ishibashi, personal interview.

[115] Russell W. Belk, *Collecting In A Consumer Society*, edited by Susan M. Pearce, (London: Routledge, 1995), pp.22.

[116] Belk, pp.24.

[117] Belk, p.24.

object'.[118] Of course, there is a counterargument to this. The first Apple computer, for instance, was built by Steve Jobs and Steve Wozniak in the late 1970s. According to CBS Boston, this original device sold for $375,000 at the Boston-based RR Auction in 2018.[119] This computer was 'industrially produced', originally selling for less than $700, and thus did not have 'the status of a uniquely crafted art-object'. Although this computer still functions as 'a commercial commodity', it was nevertheless brought to an art auction where its value soared. The computer is now interpreted as an art object and will surely be used as a 'display of wealth' by its new owner.

Speaking of fashion becoming art, between 6 June and 17 August 1997, Margiela held an exhibition at the Museum Boijmans Van Beuningen in Rotterdam in collaboration with a microbiologist[120] – one of many cases where his work has been recognised as art thanks to the concepts behind his collections. Ishibashi, however, consumes Margiela's work as commodities in his everyday life – a far cry from the 'uniquely crafted art-object' that might be exhibited in a museum. Collectors gather objects that are 'not in use anymore', preserving them in rooms or glass cases to 'display their wealth'.[121] They are consumed by being viewed. Ishibashi consumes clothes by both wearing and viewing them, but he also par-

---

[118] Fiske, p.47.

[119] CBS Boston website, *https://boston.cbslocal.com/2018/09/26/apple-1-computer-auction-sold-boston/*, (accessed on 26 September 2018).

[120] Caroline Evans, 'The Golden Dustman: A critical evaluation of the work of Martin Margiela and a review of Martin Margiela: Exhibition (9/4/1615)' in *Fashion Theory*, (London: Berg, 1998), p.73.

[121] Belk, p.25.

ticipates in the designer's creation by constructing his style and domestic space around Margiela's design philosophy. In addition, he clearly does not place his clothes and accessories in his room to 'display his wealth' – he is neither a multi-millionaire, nor an art collector per se. Here, there is a similarity to Otaku: they too consume products (action figures, posters, DVDs, and so on) and display them in their rooms, but do not do so to 'display their wealth'.

During my research, I managed to meet another Happy Victim. Seiji Kimura (see Figure 12) is an avid consumer of the Japanese fashion brand Cabane de Zucca and was featured in Volume 42 of *Happy Victims*. He lives with his wife in a two LDK room (two bedrooms, with separate living, dining and kitchen spaces). The space has a simple interior design, even though Kimura's wardrobe was cluttered.

During my interview with him, Kimura confessed that 'I did not want to be up in front of the camera to be honest with you'. However, 'I thought that this was a great opportunity to be photographed by Kyoichi Tsuzuki, one of the greatest photographers. Actually I was still hesitating whether I should accept his offer, but at the same time I did not want to end up seeing another person who would cover my place with Cabane de Zucca by rejecting his offer. I could have been jealous if I ever saw another person's collection. And this was my one and only opportunity. Had I declined Tsuzuki's offer, I would have never had a second chance'.[122] Where does Kimura's sense of jealousy come from? Jean Baudrillard is worth quoting here:

---

[122] Seiji Kimura, personal interview, (Tokyo, 18 September 2006).

Figure 12: *Happy Victims*, Volume 42, in *Ryuko Tsushin*, October 2002.

Pursuing regression to its final stage, the passion for objects climaxes in pure jealousy. Here possession derives its fullest satisfaction from the prestige the object enjoys in the eyes of other people, and the fact that they cannot have it. The jealousy complex, symptomatic of the passion of collecting at its most fanatical, can exert a proportionate influence over the reflex of ownership, even at the most innocent level.[123]

Kimura was finally featured in *Ryuko Tsushin*, not only because it was a chance for him to be captured by Tsuzuki, but also because he had a 'jealousy complex' towards a prospective owner of the same fashion brand. When I asked if he was proud to be featured in *Happy Victims*, Kimura answered clearly: 'Yes'.

---

[123] Jean Baudrillard, 'The System of Collecting', translated by Roger Cardinal in *The Cultures of Collecting*, edited by John Elsner and Roger Cardinal, (London: Reaktion Books, 1994), p.18.

Belk offers a clear definition of collecting, arguing that it is a distinct form of consumption based on acquiring obsolete items that are no longer in use.[124] Belk's definition has an interesting crossover with consumption of high-fashion items, however. 'In the collecting form of consumption, acquisition is a key process,' Belk explains. 'Someone who possesses a collection is not necessarily a collector unless they continue to acquire additional things for the collection'.[125] Although high-fashion consumers purchase new items in shops, rather than acquiring objects removed from ordinary use, they tend to keep acquiring 'additional things' from the same fashion brand each season. These garments are in ordinary use, however. If they were not, many owners would likely sell them.

THE LEGITIMISATION OF COLLECTION

With regard to how 'legitimate' an art or book collection is, Bourdieu's argument is useful. Although looking at French society, Bourdieu asserts that works of art are 'appropriate' amongst the privileged classes because these works were 'inherited from the past and deposited in museums and private collections, and also the product of history accumulated in the form of books, articles, documents, instruments, which are the trace of materialisation of theories or critiques of these theories'.[126] Therefore, works of art or theories that emerge in conjunction with these works are not 'uni-

---

[124] Belk, p.66.

[125] Belk, p.67.

[126] Bourdieu, p.228.

versal'(i.e. for all social classes), but rather for a limited number in a hierarchical society. Bourdieu states this classification in terms of appropriation of works of art:

> Because the appropriation of cultural products presupposes dispositions and competences which are not distributed universally (although they have the appearance of innateness), products are subject to exclusive appropriation, material or symbolic, and, functioning as cultural capital (objectified or internalized), they yield a profit in distinction, proportionate legitimacy, the profit par excellence, which consists in the fact of feeling justified in being (what one is), being who it is right to be.[127]

Thus, collections of art or books (first editions or prints, or those that have been signed by the author) and potentially music as well, are made up of 'exclusive' products of history and are regarded as 'legitimate' and 'excellent' due to the 'rarity' of the objects. These products function as 'cultural capital' or, as Bourdieu succinctly puts, 'the legitimate culture of class societies, a product of domination predisposed to express or legitimate domination'. Those who belong to 'legitimate culture' feel 'justified' in belonging to a certain exclusive society that is distinct from those who are in the cultures of 'little or undifferentiated' societies – they may feel they are an appropriate person to acquire historical works of art.

This is how the collection of art can be meaningfully differentiated from the collection of fashion items by young Japanese people. When I interviewed him, Tsuzuki stated that a room filled with novels or classical records might be appreciated or admired by an audience; on the other hand, they might find it funny to see a

---

[127] Bourdieu, p.228.

small studio flat filled with high-fashion clothes and accessories.[128] It would not be surprising if some of the audience for *Happy Victims* considered the fashion consumers silly for choosing to live in a small space in order to afford more clothes. This lifestyle may be interpreted as less intellectual than that of art collectors. Many of the items the Happy Victims consume are 'expensive' and some pieces are 'rare' – when they appear in public, they may look 'legitimate' and 'excellent'. However, Tsuzuki's subjects also revealed their living spaces (highlighting their social class) which create the opposite impression. Readers may wonder whether the Happy Victims are actually 'appropriate' owners of these high fashion items and the 'cultural capital' they represent.

If I refer to Bourdieu's view, art is the product of a 'history' that is exclusively appropriate to a limited number of people, whereas fashion items are more appropriate to wider social classes. Louis Vuitton, Prada and Gucci have physical stores around the world, as well as an online presence. Their price points vary across smartphone cases, trainers, handbags, ready-to-wear garments and couture – a deliberate strategy to generate sales from a wide range of social classes. Although some high-fashion items are very expensive and could function as 'cultural capital', others are comparatively affordable. Even if you are not from a wealthy family, and are a salaryman or a student (i.e. those in 'little or undifferentiated' societies), by saving up it is still possible to buy some high-fashion items. Could you do the same in order to acquire 'legitimate' works of art? Only a few years after fashion items are sold, they typically become less valuable as secondhand items.

---

[128] Tsuzuki, personal interview.

Perhaps the fashion collections that some salarymen or students possess may eventually be 'legitimate' in Bordieu's sense of the term as time goes by. For example, items designed by Margiela himself (he resigned from his own brand in 2009) are now sold on the auction website *1stdibs*, while in 2019 the Victoria & Albert Museum in London held *Inside Christian Dior: Designers of Dreams*, an exhibition of Dior's work which highlighted how such garments are now untouchable for the average consumer. Fashion brands change from time to time as designers come and go. Even if a brand carries the same name throughout its lifespan, its products may vary dramatically between periods. As such, fashion items designed by a particular designer can become more valuable as time passes. It is not dissimilar to how works of art by deceased artists tend to be worth more at auction than those by living practitioners.

THE INTERNET - ONE OF THE PRIMARY SOURCES FOR THE DEVELOPMENT OF OTAKU CULTURE

In 1993, the infrastructure for domestic internet use began to put in place in Japan, and in 1995 providers such as Infoweb, Asahi Net and Yahoo! were founded.[129] While Otaku culture had developed before this period, the internet revolution contributed to it immensely. I will demonstrate this by describing *Ni Channel*, a website through which Otaku could share information.

The proliferation of the internet has enabled millions of people to share knowledge and experiences in a way that was previ-

---

[129] Hara, p.82.

ously impossible. It is also a useful source to explain the Nomura Research Institute's third definition of Otaku ('They have profound knowledge of the particular category of consumer goods, in which they often develop creatively and share with others'), in conjunction with Fiske's analysis of fan culture. Fiske says that there is a category of fan productivity called 'textual productivity', which is created by fans based on 'the official culture'.[130] A good example is how '*Star Trek* fans... wrote full-length novels filling in the syntagmatic gaps in the original narrative' before circulating 'these novels, and other writings, among themselves through an extensive distribution network'.[131] This, of course, took place in the pre-internet period – their network must have been much more limited than nowadays.

Ni Channel has been popular in Japan since launching in May 1999, enabling people to share a wide range of information about politics, the economy, science, celebrity gossip, animation, TV, music, food, and art and design (the list goes on).[132] *Ni Channel* is a chat board where people can freely write about anything, and is a source for comment and news which you could never find in newspapers, magazines or TV shows (although there is fake news on *Ni Channel* too). The website also has a section for fashion, where fans produce texts for pleasure. Fiske goes on to say:

> There is also a difference in circulation; because fan texts are not produced for profit, they do not need to be mass-marketed, so unlike offi-

---

[130] Fiske, p.30.

[131] Fiske, p.39.

[132] Ni Channel, *http://www.2ch.net*, (accessed on 5 December 2006).

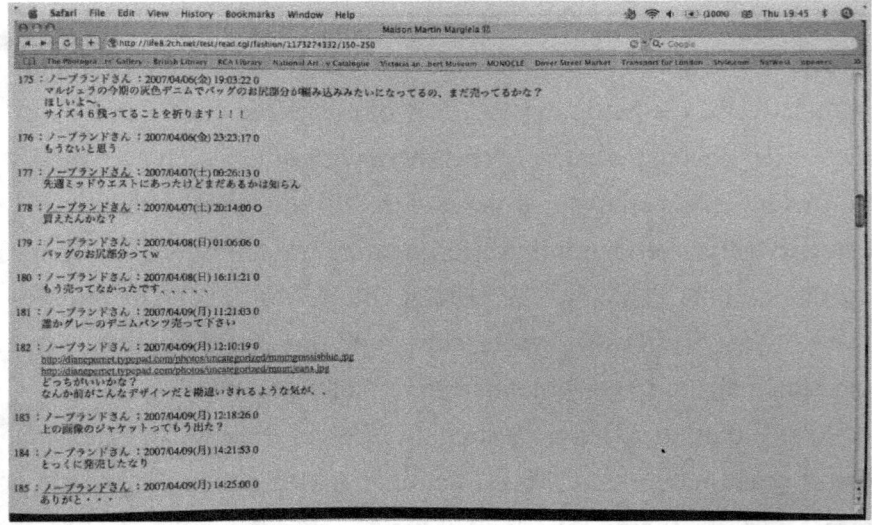

Figure 13: The Martin Margiela bulletin board on *Ni Channel*.

cial culture, fan culture makes no attempt to circulate its texts outside its own community. They are 'narrowcast', not broadcast, texts.[133]

Ni Channel attracted an audience because a lot of information published on the website was not broadcast, but only 'narrowcast'. If you look at *Ni Channel*, there are around 700 threads in the fashion section. It includes a variety of fashion brands, from high-fashion to high street. On the Martin Margiela thread (See Figure 13), for instance, people (all writing anonymously) share their knowledge about how to behave in the brand's shops and when they can expect to see a specific item in stock:

175: **No Brand-san**: 2007/04/06 (Fri) 19:03:22
Are the Margiela's grey jeans with its woven details on the hip still in stock? I really want them! I do hope they still have the size 46.

---

[133] Fiske, p.39.

176: **No Brand-san**: 2007/04/06 (Fri) 23:23:17
I don't think they do anymore.
177: **No Brand-san**: 2007/04/07 (Sat) 00:26:13
I saw them in Midwest last week but don't know if they are still there…
178: **No Brand-san**: 2007/04/07 (Sat) 20:14:00
Did you manage to buy the jeans?
179: **No Brand-san**: 2007/04/08 (Sun) 01:06:06
Woven hip lol
180: **No Brand-san**: 2007/04/08 (Sun) 16:11:21
They did not have them anymore…
181: **No Brand-san**: 2007/04/09 (Mon) 11:21:03
Can someone sell me the pair of grey jeans?

191: **No Brand-san**: 2007/04/09 (Mon) 14:58:44
>181 I found them in ISETAN today.

195: **No Brand-san**: 2007/04/10 (Tue) 17:56:32
I pass by the Margiela's shop every time I go to the ramen noodle stand in Ebisu. Can I enter the shop, although my fashion style is quite Americana?

198: **No Brand-san**: 2007/04/10 (Tue) 18:13:10
It is no problem. Margiela does not discriminate people because of that.
199: **No Brand-san**: 2007/04/10 (Tue) 23:34:21
If you have a poker face, that is fine. If you do not behave cool, you would be ignored.

This is an example of 'narrowcast' text production. The person who missed the opportunity to buy a pair of Margiela jeans was desperately asking for help from other Margiela fans about where they could find them. Another person who had never visited the Margiela shop was unsure if their usual outfit was suitable for entering the shop. Other invisible individuals gave advice in response. These texts are not produced for any commercial purposes, nor targeted at a mass audiences. This fits exactly with what Fiske argues about how 'fan culture' circulates textual productivity. It is also noteworthy that *Ni Channel*, thanks to its breadth of content, enabled both Otaku and fashion fans to exist on the same platform – something which had not been the case in the 1980s.

These online and offline communications are no longer a problem of 'reality' and 'virtuality'. Daniel Miller and Don Slater discuss this matter by raising the example of internet use in Trinidad,stating that 'the internet is not a monolithic or placeless cyberspace; rather, it is numerous new technologies, used by diverse people, in diverse real-world locations'.[134] In comparison to face-to-face communication, the internet might be assumed to be 'unreal', but it is intimately linked to daily life. Cyberspace has blurred the boundaries of 'reality' and 'virtuality'. As a result it has expanded the way we communicate. Miller and Slater continue:

> The internet has both produced new freedoms (of information and of speech) and come to stand as a symbol of potential freedoms. Indeed, two quite contrasting notions of libertarianism have been closely linked to the Internet, one from free-market ideologies of neoliberalism, the other, 'net-libertarianism' from post modernism.[135]

Although Miller and Slater focus this idea on the internet revolution in Trinidad, it can also be applied to Japan, where *Ni Channel* has shown how 'free-market ideologies' and 'net libertarianism' link to the internet. People who are online are able to acquire and leave information in a particular chat space. These activities result in consumption of a text by anonymous users who

---

[134] Daniel Miller and Don Slater, *The Internet: An Ethnographic Approach*, (Oxford: Berg, 2000), p.1.

[135] Miller and Slater, p.16.

see this information. They have acquired a 'freedom' of communication.

This links to Fiske's argument in terms of 'offcial' and 'unofficial' culture. Miller and Slater argue that many elements arising from the internet should be understood not as freedom versus constraint, but as conflict between different models of order and normativity. They go on to say that 'much internet use involves decentralisation and diffusion of authority and power, and hence challenges to both hierarchical organisational models and those whose interests are vested in them'.[136] Information about 'the official culture' that consists of 'authority and power' has been decentralised and diffused in 'placeless' locations by anonymous people. We are no longer entirely dependant on the 'authority and power' of traditional TV or radio stations, which centralised information sources. Now, anyone can create a platform to share unique sources in 'placeless' locations with people you would never meet in your life.

Miller and Slater forecasted the expansion of the internet: 'It (the internet) may be its very novelty that makes it an ideal idiom for imagining the future. After a while it is quite possible that it will become more mundane and taken for granted'.[137] This prediction, made in 2000 was right – today, it is very difficult to imagine our lives and businesses without the internet.

---

[136] Miller and Slater, p.18.

[137] Miller and Slater, p.14.

Chapter Three
Japanese Homes

BREACHING THE PUBLIC/PRIVATE DISTINCTION

In this chapter, I will explore how we might consider the apartments that belong to the Happy Victims. What is the relationship – spatial, economic and social – between the spaces as homes and the spaces as sites of the Happy Victims' collections? This means exploring the setting itself. What constitutes a Japanese home?

Chapter One addressed the problem of the minimalist aesthetics of Japanese architecture and domestic interiors, explaining how Tsuzuki's aesthetic revealed the real, cluttered living conditions of young Japanese people. My analysis in this chapter focuses on the separation of public and private in the home. I will also explore traditional family life and familial roles in the home as opposed to the individual lives lived by the Happy Victims.

I have selected Krishan Kumar's essay 'Home: The Promise and Predicament of Private Life at the End of the Twentieth Century' to provide a definition of the distinction between the public and private in the home. His text, published in 1997, sets out the idea of the European home as a kind of ideal, rather than representing just one example of the social and material culture of home constitution. Drawing on my background, I would like to consider what distinguishes the Japanese homes that emerged during and after the 1990s from other types of home in Europe, and from other types of home within Japanese society. Kumar's definitions, albeit idealised, are useful for drawing out some of the specific characteristics of the Happy Victims' homes. I will also make some comparisons with Inge Maria Daniels's text 'The Untidy Japanese House' which deals with traditional Japanese homes, to address what kind of material culture may distinguish the Happy Victims' homes.

As I discussed in the Introduction, Tsuzuki's *Tokyo Style* showed that contemporary Japanese dwellings are by no means as minimal as European and American scholars seem to think. Instead, they may be small, cluttered and full of objects – not at all what Zen philosophy might prescribe. Both *Tokyo Style* and *Happy Victims* are relevant to this chapter in investigating 'real' modern Japanese living conditions; Tsuzuki's works show that as long as his subjects' could consume what they wanted, they were happy with their lives, no matter how small and cluttered their spaces were.

Tsuzuki's works also provoke consideration of the notion of public and private within Japanese houses, for his photography publicly exposes his subjects in their nominally private spaces. Are the public and private clearly separated in such a case? It is also worth investigating the independence of Tsuzuki's inhabitants – the majority do not cohabit with their families, but instead spend most of their time alone in their rooms.

In Tsuzuki's photographs for *Ryuko Tsushin*, readers are granted access to around 90 rooms. As I discussed in Chapter One, *Happy Victims* was an unusual series in the history of Japanese fashion magazines (in fact, fashion magazines globally) because Tsuzuki stepped into his subjects' private rooms in order to show their clutter. Had Tsuzuki not embarked on the project, we might never have had the opportunity to explore or understand the kind of living and consumption practices it represented (and this book would never have existed).

However, following their representation in Tsuzuki's work are these spaces still protected and private? The Happy Victims opened their private spaces to the mass readership of the magazine, thereby transforming them into public spaces – at least in some sense of the term. I would like to define public and private by referencing Philippe Ariès's text 'The Family and the City in the Old World and the New'. Ariès's definition is based on the Industrial Revolution in Western society, although his archetype of public and private segmentation has changed as the boundaries between the two have blurred. Ariès states that public space (that is, the working world) is subject to 'strict surveillance', whereas private space (that is, the family home) is 'a place of refuge' free from outside control. As Ariès goes on to say, 'Thus, the separation of space into work areas and living areas corresponds to the division of life into public sector and private sector. The family falls within the private sector'.[138] This clear separation of public and private, however, may be challenging in modern Japan, especially for my case studies.

Each volume of *Happy Victims* features an accompanying text by Tsuzuki, which introduces the subject's lifestyle. Given this information, we have more or less 'invaded' their space – could this be a kind of voyeurism? Certainly, Tsuzuki has commented that he experienced a sense of voyeurism when he took the photographs.[139] However, what is 'voyeurism' in the case of the Happy Victims? Should it be understood as the instinct of the photographer who wishes to find practices or meanings that are otherwise hidden or obscure? Or is it to be regarded as 'scopophilia', a term which describes the intimate pleasure of looking and which carries

---

[138] Phillipe Ariès, 'The Family and the City in the Old World and the New' in *Changing Images of the Family*, edited by Virginia Tufte and Barbara Meyerhoff, (London: Yale University Press, 1979), p.33.

[139] Tsuzuki, personal interview.

strong connotations of erotic desire or a sense of taboo? This matter is complicated by the fact that the Happy Victims are precisely that – 'happy' to be subject to our scrutiny.

Viviana Narotzky's text 'Dream Homes and DIY: television, new media and the domestic makeover' in *Imagined Interiors* is a useful source for this. Narotzky argues that the boundaries of public and private in homes have been breached by the media (television and internet), which allows spectators into private rooms to experience the pleasure of looking into other people's lives. One example of this phenomenon is the TV programme *Changing Rooms*, which originally ran from 1996 to 2004 on the BBC. According to Narotzky's text 'The programme features two neighbouring couples, redecorating each other's space under the guidance of an interior designer within a fixed, limited budget'.[140] The programme attracted around 12m viewers,[141] but Narotzky points out the 'paradox' of home makeover shows of this kind:

> On the one hand, the hosts engage in conversation with the homeowners whose rooms are being redecorated… On the other, these programmes transgress the boundaries of the home, intruding on the intimacy of the domestic environment by subjecting it to the gaze of millions of viewers from the privacy of their own living rooms. This paradox of public intimacy underpins the voyeur's pleasure, which reality television has made safely available to all.[142]

---

[140] Viviana Narotzky, 'Dream Homes and DIY: television, new media and the domestic makeover' in *Imagined Interiors*, (London: V&A Publications, 2006), p.258.

[141] Narotzky, p.258.

[142] Narotzky, p.267.

This argument is pertinent to *Happy Victims*, even if the series was published in a different media. Tsuzuki revealed fashion-obsessed people's private spaces to the public, photographing and interviewing each inhabitant (similar to the way in which the hosts of *Changing Rooms* were filmed in conversation with the homeowners), and recording these conversations in his texts. When published, everybody featured in *Happy Victims* was subjected to the gaze of around 150,000 spectators in Japan, meaning that Tsuzuki blurred the boundaries of public and private by intruding on the intimate domestic space of his subjects. He gave readers a 'voyeur's pleasure', feeding their curiosity while simultaneously satisfying any need for publicity a Victim might feel.

Roland Barthes illustrates how photographs expose the private to the public. In his book *Camera Lucida*, Barthes states:

> Each photograph is read as the private appearance of its referent: the age of photography corresponds precisely to the explosion of the private into the public, or rather into the creation of a new social value, which is the publicity of the private: the private is consumed as such, publicly.[143]

It seems clear that photographs can reveal 'the private appearance' to the public, which may result in 'a new social value', and that talented photographers such as Sander and Tsuzuki have embarked on original projects that explode the private into the public, where it can be consumed by the gaze of spectators. These photographers were able to offer a new interpretation of social classes, structures,

---

[143] Roland Barthes, *Camera Lucida* translated by Richard Howard, (London: Jonathan Cape, 1982), p.98.

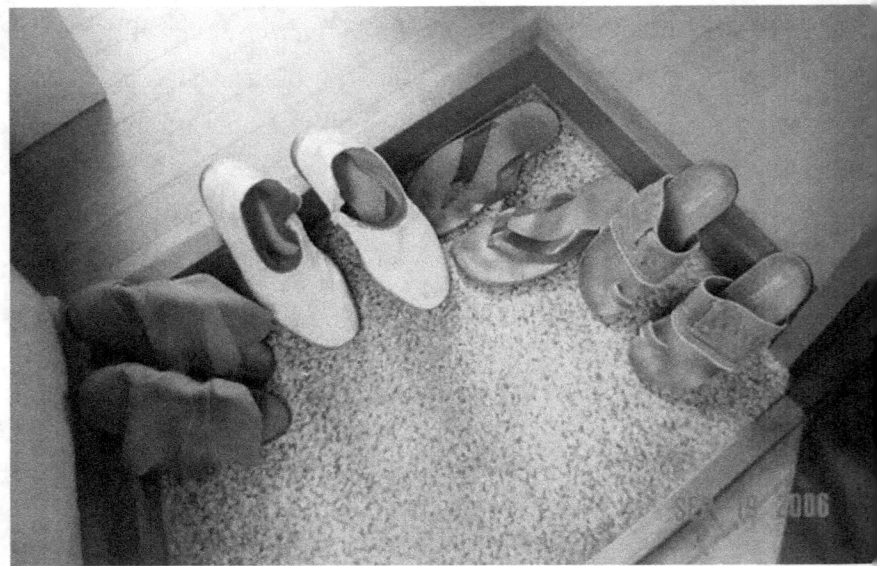

Figure 14: The genkan in Ishibashi's house. The dark panel in the bottom right is the front door. All the shoes are by Martin Margiela.

and realities of living. Photographs educate as well as giving pleasure, hence increasing our understanding of other worlds.

A TRADITIONAL ELEMENT INHERITED BY THE MODERN JAPANESE HOME

As has been established, somebody who has been depicted in a publication may not possess their 'private' space anymore. If the Happy Victims still possess their sense of the boundary between public and private space, is this based on the Japanese architectural tradition, ritual or something else? Furthermore, is the Japanese sense of the public/private distinction different from the European sense? All modern Japanese houses have a genkan, a square space where shoes are taken off after entering the space (Figure 14). It is an element inherited from traditional houses, providing the space onto which you are supposed to step onto before walking on the floor of the house or room it demarcates.

Traditional Japanese houses feature tatami mats, which people want to keep clean by avoiding walking on them with shoes. In the 17th century, Samurai began setting up genkan at the entrances of their houses as a result of the influence of local monks who took their shoes off before entering the temple. Monks already had the concept of a boundary between the 'public', which could be polluted (at the time, footpaths were often dusty), and the 'private', which was a sacred space and therefore kept hygienic at all times.[144] To Japanese people, therefore, this particular place and the action of taking off their shoes has come to mark the boundary of public and private spaces. The genkan is one of the main elements that differentiates these two spaces in Japan from the West.

Takeshi Nakagawa, a Japanese historian of architecture, states that the kutsunugi-ishi or shoe-removing stone (Figure 15) was commonly set up in traditional Japanese houses 'as a step between an earthen floor at ground level and the raised floor of a structure'.[145] Nakagawa explains:

> Clearly, the Kutsunugi-ishi was developed to suit a custom peculiar to Japanese living space, i.e., changing one's footwear on entering and leaving the house, and the structuring that this requires. It is a site where one performs certain actions on moving between the indoors and

---

[144] Mitsuru Oki, *Everyday French*, (Tokyo: NHK Publishing, 2014), pp.110-111.

[145] Takeshi Nakagawa, *The Japanese House: space, memory and language*, (Tokyo: the International House of Japan, Inc., 2005), p.26.

Figure 15: Kutsunugi-ishi. Courtesy of Kouganji temple website.

outdoors, and a device that one uses in those actions; at the same time, it connotes both the heterogeneity of the interior and exterior spaces and the relationship between them, in other words, their boundary.[146]

The kutsunugi-ishi has been transformed into the modern genkan. The ritual of removing and leaving your shoes in a common place before stepping onto a floor is still important in Japan – therefore, it is an intrinsic design feature in Japanese houses. This is significant for Japanese people, as well as foreign scholars who focus on Japanese homes, in that it not only evokes cleanliness, but also a certain boundary between the public and private.

---

[146] Nakagawa, p.26.

EUROPEAN AND JAPANESE NOTIONS OF PUBLIC/PRIVATE IN THE IDENTIFICATION OF THE SELF

I would like to challenge a notion of 'public' and 'private' that has been suggested by a number of European scholars. In Krishan Kumar's essay 'Home: The Promise and Predicament of Private Life at the End of the Twentieth Century', he positions 'the home' in modern life, stating:

> It [the home] is the place with which individuals can most readily identify and it easily lends itself to the symbolic expression of personal identity… It is the place where the self can be expressed outside of social roles… It is the private realm in an increasingly public and intrusive world.[147]

The readers of *Ryuko Tsushin* were able to observe each Happy Victim's 'principal source of identity and personal fulfilment'.[148] More precisely, what the spectators observe is a representation of this, as captured by Tsuzuki's lens. If we recognise the internal spaces of a home as being completely segregated from the outside world (which may not always be the case in this world of photography, video and social media contents), how private or secure would the inhabitants feel? Generally speaking, each Happy Victim decorates their room with objects that bear a relation to their interests (a poster of their favourite musician, an athlete or a

---

[147] Krishan Kumar, 'Home: The Promise and Predicament of Private Life at the End of the Twentieth Century' in *Public And Private In Thought And Practice*, edited by Jeff Weinstraub and Krishan Kumar, (Chicago: University of Chicago Press, 1997), p.207.

[148] Kumar, p.206.

film, for example) or what they do for living (such as instruments for musicians, books for students, records for DJs, and so forth). These objects all represent or imply their owners' 'social roles'. The inhabitants express their social roles through these symbolic objects, which are 'the principal source of identity' in their rooms. Thus, few people can escape their social roles, even in their private spaces. If a person is a PR manager, for example, whether consciously or unconsciously they will likely still imply their identity in their room by accommodating objects relevant to their job (perhaps they display a number of objects they have fallen in love with after promoting them for work).

Narotzky's point of view is useful to illustrate my argument. Narotzky points out that *Changing Rooms* contributed to the idea of domestic decoration as an expression of personal aesthetics. She continues by saying 'throughout the twentieth century, the idea of the home as a site of social reform, the good home as Utopian project, has been contending with the idea of domestic space as an expression of middle-class taste and an emotional sanctuary'.[149] Although the people who participated in the programme were largely drawn from the English middle classes, Narotzky's argument is adaptable to those captured by Tsuzuki's camera because the nature of their occupations makes them equivalent in class. Narotzyky also states:

> By your home you shall be judged. Our living rooms are us, our kitchens are an expression of what (we) want to say about

---

[149] Narotzky, p.267.

(ourselves)... We are all creative, taste is a democratic commodity, we can all do it ourselves...[150]

No matter which class a person belongs to – what kind of occupation they are in – they 'shall be judged' by their domestic space, especially if that space is represented to the public via media. The taste of a room's inhabitant is judged by the commodities displayed in their domestic space. Within budgetary constraints, everybody can express creativity and embark on DIY domestic decoration to express their identity. In the case of the Happy Victims, the spectators would judge the inhabitants primarily by their choice of fashion brand, the quantity of garments, and how they dressed in their photo, rather than their commodities. Even if they could not afford something they wanted to display in order to fully express their aesthetic or encapsulate who they were, they were 'Happy' with their rooms as they were – their priority was always to spend most of their disposable income on fashion items.

In this context, Bourdieu's theory of taste is useful. According to Bourdieu, 'taste is what brings together things and people that go together'.[151] In a system of class differentiation, people express their status through 'clothing, pronunciation, bearing, posture, manners'. Each factor takes on its own meaning and value in relation to each person in the system. This kind of mutual reinforcement between a person and their choice of commodities partially constitutes that person's place in the social structure.[152]

---

[150] Narotzky, p.271.

[151] Bourdieu, p.241.

[152] Bourdieu, p.243.

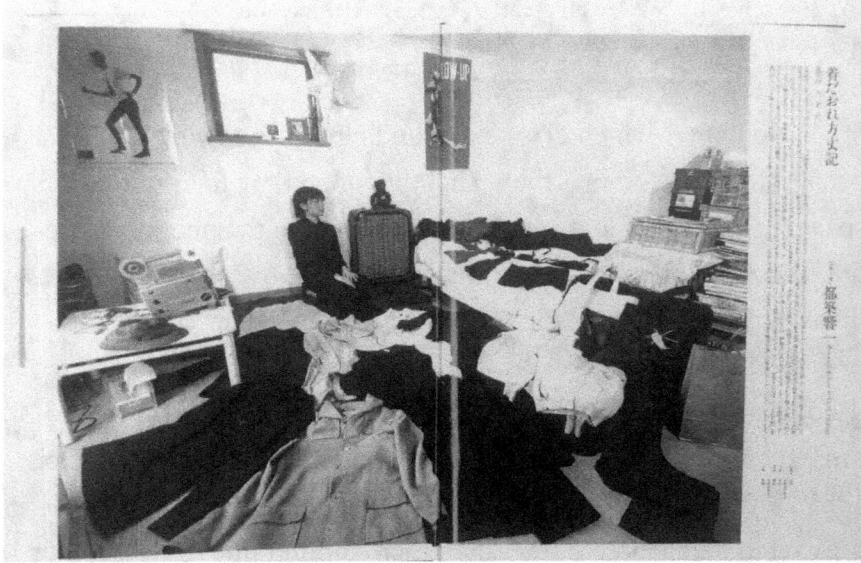

Figure 16: *Happy Victims*, Volume 37, featuring an A.P.C. consumer in *Ryuko Tsushin*, July 2002.

With this in mind, a question emerges about Kumar's argument. The inhabitants in Tsuzuki's series seem to express their 'personal culture', not only through the objects they love, but also through their understanding of their social identity, or 'social role' as Kumar puts it. For instance, the manager of a fashion boutique decorates his room with items or promotional posters (which are often very beautiful) from their store. A fashion media director places a film projector in her room (Figure 16). Given that the Happy Victims chose to live in small rooms, however, they would not have had much storage for such things. Here we can see the inhabitant's 'creativity' – if they cannot store and hide their film

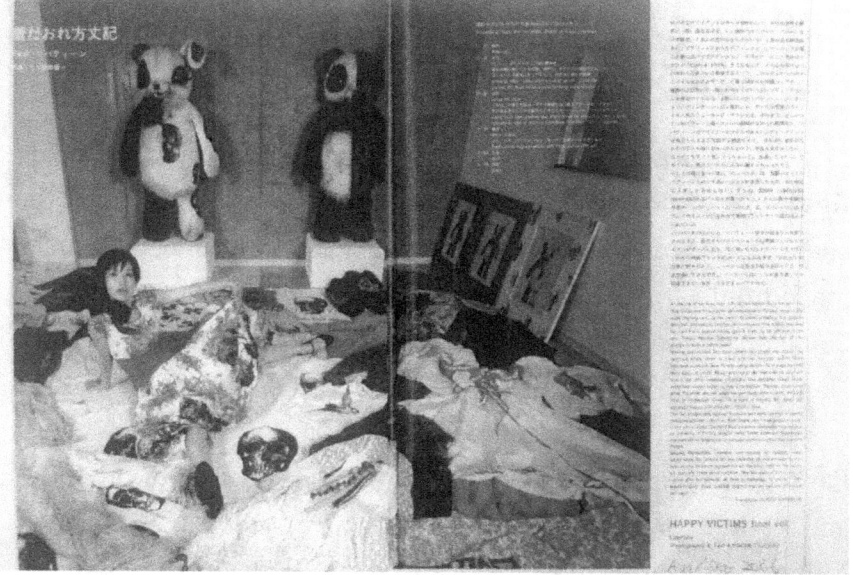

Figure 17: *Happy Victims*, Final Volume, in *Ryuko Tsushin*, August & September double issue, 2006.

projector, why not display it? According to the accompanying text, the Victim actually enjoys running a home theatre.[153]

Another Happy Victim who kindly accepted my request for an interview was Nagi Noda (Figure 17), an internationally successful artist who featured in Jonathan Ross's *Japanorama* in 2006. Featured in the final volume of Tsuzuki's series in 2006, Noda was obsessed with the fashion brand Libertine. Being a commercially successful artist, Noda was by no means an ordinary consumer. According to Tsuzuki's text about Noda:

> Never previously did she take to any one brand, but after meeting Libertine's solo designer Cindy Green when she visited Japan, it was a

---

[153] Tsuzuki, *Happy Victims*, Volume 37, *Ryuko Tsushin* (Tokyo: INFAS Publications, July 2002), pp.141-142.

revelation. 'Neither of us knew what the other did, but when we saw each other's work, we both took an immediate liking'. Now best of friends, Ms. Noda just naturally began collecting Ms. Green's brand.[154]

Noda decorates her living room with statues of Hanpanda, a figure she made in collaboration with Libertine. Noda created this character in both two and three dimensions. Hanpanda is a panda made from various materials, half of which is executed in one colour, half another ('han' means 'half' in Japanese). The two Hanpandas in Noda's home are special editions, of which there are only three in the world – the other was bought by someone in Paris.[155] Noda became commercially successful with the character, and worked for global companies such as Coca Cola, Nike and Monoprix on their advertising campaigns. Hanpanda symbolises her 'social role'. It seems Noda's 'public' and 'private' were mixed up – what she did was what she loved, and therefore it was natural for her to display the figures she created, and of which she was proud, in her room. Perhaps she did not often switch off from work, even in her room. What she created came from who she was and her passion was to create such figures and visions. But is this particular to Noda, or does this apply to all of the Happy Victims? Did they project a sense of the boundaries between public and private or were they mixed up as well?

Christena E. Nippert-Eng's argument in her book *Home and Work* illustrates this problem. Nippert-Eng says that there are 'typifications of the ways we classify and juxtapose items, acts,

---

[154] Tsuzuki, *Happy Victims*, Final Volume, *Ryuko Tsushin* (Tokyo: INFAS Publications, August and September 2006), pp.143-144.

[155] Tsuzuki, p.143.

thoughts, and aspects of self to accommodate social and personal expectations', which are called 'integration' and 'segmentation'.[156] This is a highly conceptual matter, for 'home' and 'work' are 'experiential realms' for each person. For instance, people who work at home, or who talk about their work a lot, or who take their children to their workplace, should possess a sense of integration that transcends the boundaries of home and work. On the other hand, those who have a sense of segmentation tend to draw a clear line between the two by not talking to their colleagues about their family, or by separating their outfits for home and work. Therefore, 'the more we integrate, the more the problematic part of our boundary work tends to focus on boundary placement... The more we segment, then, the more attention focuses on transcendent boundary work'.[157]

Noda made an interesting comment about showing her space: 'it could be an invasion of my privacy if I had to show my bedroom, but I did not mind showing my living room in the magazine'.[158] Is this because she presents her artistic work in her living room and somehow has a sense of that space being 'public'? Noda integrates the boundary between home and work, but still seems to draw a barrier between public and private. Regarding this, I would like to quote Nippert-Eng:

> Frames (home/work) become activated in the form of 'mentalities', ways of thinking and being when we're mentally and/or physically 'in'

---

[156] Christena E. Nippert-Eng, *Home and Work* (Chicago: The University of Chicago Press, 1995), p.17.

[157] Nippert-Eng, p.27.

[158] Nagi Noda, personal interview, (Tokyo, 26 August 2006).

either place. It's the invocation of a particular mentality that imbues otherwise subjectively meaningless places, things, times of day, tasks at hand, and role relations with their experiential significance. If we think in pretty much the same way, feel like pretty much the same person, and go about our activities and interactions in much the same frame of mind, paying attention to the same kinds of things and having similar expectations of those around us no matter where we are, we have a more continuous, more integrated experience of home and work. If, on the other hand, we find ourselves feeling like two different people, acting out two different personae, approaching our activities with different perspectives, and interpreting what others do differently at home and work, we have a more segmented experience of these realms.[159]

In Nippert-Eng's schema, Noda is clearly more integrated – she would have felt the same person at work as at home. Nippert-Eng goes on: 'Through the ways we manage our selves, objects, people, thoughts, and tasks, we not only concretize mental boundaries but our mental journeys over them'.[160] Noda's 'mental journey' through herself, objects (such as Hanpandas), people (Tsuzuki, when he photographed her), thoughts (her creativity) and tasks (her work) integrated her public and private spaces. At the same time, she segregated public and private by her own standards – her 'mental boundaries'.

Noda was an internationally established artist whose name was clearly included in the article – by contrast, many of Tsuzuki's other subjects preferred to remain anonymous despite agreeing to be photographed and described in the magazine. We might say that Noda is, in a way, marketing herself as a 'product' by being exposed in the media. When I look at Noda in Tsuzuki's photograph,

---

[159] Nippert-Eng, pp.26-27.

[160] Nippert-Eng, pp.27-28.

it seems like she is performing. Noda's eyes look straight into the camera, and her left arm picks up the bottom of the dress she is wearing (perhaps she chose this particular dress to create a colour contrast against the background – there are many others laid out on the floor). Meanwhile, she supports her body with her right arm, while her legs are spread with her shoes still on – an unusual thing to do in a Japanese domestic space. Perhaps she wanted to dress as she does when she goes outside, indicating that she integrates her home and work. It looks as if Noda had planned the picture prior to the photoshoot (this was, after all, the nature of her job) – the way in which she is holding her body appears to be choreographed, as if she was posing to be provocative and also to show her affection and respect for Cindy Green of Libertine. By contrast, the majority of Tsuzuki's subjects were unsure about what to do before and during the photoshoot, and therefore appear quite stiff. If my interpretation is correct, was Noda using her living room as a stage to perform? Regarding this analysis, it is wise to quote sociologist Erving Goffman, who published *The Presentation of Self in Everyday Life*. Goffman opens his introduction as follows:

> When an individual enters the presence of others, they commonly seek to acquire information about him or to bring into play information about him already possessed. They will be interested in his general socio-economic status, his conception of self, his attitude towards them, his competence, his trustworthiness, etc. Although some of this information seems to be sought almost as an end in itself, there are usually quite practical reasons for acquiring it. Information about the individual helps to define the situation, enabling others to know in advance what he will expect of them and what they may expect of him. Informed in

these ways, the others will know how best to act in order to call forth a desired response from him.[161]

This coincides with what we (Noda, Tsuzuki, the magazine and all its readers) do in order to understand and analyse the individual who appears in the photograph. When someone appears in front of others, the viewer tends to form an impression of that person based on their facial expression or the way they speak, and so forth. The person being viewed may, in addition to this, want people to think highly of them.[162] 'A Performance', according to Goffman, is what may occur in all areas of social life; 'all the activity of a given participant on a given occasion which serves to influence in any way any of the other participants'.[163] Noda gives us information about herself (her socio-economic status, her creativity and attitude) through her 'performance', and in return we provide the desired response (admiration or respect, perhaps). Goffman also states the importance of 'a setting' in which the individual influences the observers:

> First, there is the 'setting', involving furniture, décor, physical layout, and other background items which supply the scenery and stage props for the spate of human action played out before, within, or upon it. A setting tends to stay put, geographically speaking, so that those who would use a particular setting as part of their performance cannot begin

---

[161] Ervin Goffman, *The Presentation of Self in Everyday Life*, (New York, Penguin Books, 1990), p.13.

[162] Goffman, p.15.

[163] Goffman, p.26.

their act until they have brought themselves to the appropriate place and must terminate their performance when they leave it.[164]

No one can project their self without 'a setting'. In Noda's case, her living room – decorated as it is with the statues of Hanpanda and Libertine – is the 'appropriate place' to begin her performance. To expose herself with her work is a means of self-promotion (public), although the setting was her living room (private, in theory) and her 'performance' terminated when Tsuzuki finished the photo shoot and left her living room. These phrases apply not only to the rooms in Tsuzuki's photographs, but also rooms in general. Even if photographs of a room are not published, by allowing them to be taken the room's owner invites a guest into their space (which does not often happen in Tokyo, due to limited space) and in so doing projects their self by being observed in a setting – a space which is surrounded by objects that differentiate the room's owner from visitors. This kind of performance results from the impression an inhabitant would like to make on viewers. Goffman goes on:

> When an individual appears before others his actions will influence the definition of the situation which they come to have. Sometimes the individual will act in a thoroughly calculating manner, expressing himself in a given way solely in order to give the kind of impression to others that is likely to evoke from them a specific response he is concerned to obtain. Sometimes the individual will be calculating in his activity but be relatively unaware that this is the case.[165]

---

[164] Goffman, p.33.

[165] Goffman, p.17.

This fits the photograph of Noda perfectly. Although Goffman acknowledges that an 'individual [may] be calculating in his activity' while still being 'relatively unaware', Noda's case seems different to many of the other Happy Victims. While they may be highly aware of the 'specific response' they are likely to receive from others, Noda seems especially 'calculating' in terms of what media exposure means to her as an artist. She must have been aware of how her clients' would see the photograph, and it is also possible that she managed to position (or reinforce) herself as a celebrity by presenting Green as her best friend. Ishibashi is not dissimilar – he projects an image of himself by wearing Margiela from head to toe, not only in the photograph taken in his home, but also in the Bunka Fashion College. He must be aware of 'the impression to others that [he] is likely to evoke from them'. Ishibashi also seems to have blurred the boundary between public and private – happily surrounded by Margiela items and speculating about outfit rotations, he slept in the small room every day (private), with this existence inextricably interwoven with what he did at work (public).

THE TRADITIONAL AND MODERN HOME

Are the homes of the Happy Victims typical homes? What might this mean in the Japanese context? If traditional Japanese homes are based on principals different to those established in contemporary Japanese homes, then the Tokyo homes of the Happy Victims mark a departure from tradition. In this section, I will demonstrate the differences between the consumer behaviour and material culture of a typical family and the *Happy Victims* by referencing Inge Maria Daniels's work.

In a family home (whether bought or rented), each member of the household possesses a role. Traditionally in Japan, these roles are familiar – husband, wife and children. The husband is supposed to work outside the home and make money. If the wife is a full-time housewife, she is meant to take care of the household and organise the home. Children should receive their education from both school and their parents. Although clearly restrictive, for many this remains the common image of a typical Japanese family.

This kind of family was investigated by Daniels, who carried out field research in two houses in Japan. One of them, the Miyada family house, is a two-storey detached building with a historical lineage of more than 100 years. The house is located on a small island in Hiroshima. It is very old and traditional, although an adjacent house has been turned into a modern annex to accommodate the Miyadas' three children. Therefore, the house is a combination of both traditional and modern elements.

Daniels's essay addresses the social roles of each family member. Mr. Miyada is the fifth successive president of the company where he works, while Mrs. Miyada is a full-time housewife with a strict schedule for shopping, cleaning and cooking.[166] Each individual has a defined 'social role',[167] even in the confines of their private space.

---

[166] Inge Maria Daniels, 'The Untidy Japanese House' in *Home Possessions*, edited by Daniel Miller, (New York: Berg, 2001), p.212.

[167] Kumar, p.207.

Perhaps we need to reconsider whether Kumar's argument fits Japanese homes or the Japanese sense of public and private. Japanese people have always, to one degree or another, expressed their personal or social identity through objects in their rooms, which are based on their understanding of good taste. Daniels emphasises this point, with another case study of the Moris family home:

> The Moris [family] create their familial identity with elements of Japanese aesthetics such as tatami rooms and tea sets, but other items of material culture such as abstract art, a piano, French wine and electrical appliances carry similar importance. This is another piece of evidence that supports the argument that 'Japanese' and 'Western' should be seen as different consumer choices which can be easily mixed.[168]

This brings me to one of Tsuzuki's Happy Victims, whose tatami room is filled with Jean Paul Gaultier clothes (Figure 18). The room is a traditional Japanese space owned by an accessory designer who has had presentations in Paris. The inhabitant remains anonymous. The interior looks simple, and she has decorated a mannequin bust with her accessories. This decoration indicates her occupation – her 'outside social role' – while she is also a wife to her husband, who is an Enka producer (a genre of melodramatic Japanese popular music).[169] Her room's material culture represents what Daniels describes as an idea in which 'Japanese and Western should be seen as different consumer choices which can be easily mixed'. Traditionally, this type of room would have

---

[168] Daniels, p.216.

[169] Tsuzuki, *Happy Victims*, Volume 10, *Ryuko Tsushin* (Tokyo: INFAS Publications, March 1999), p.130-131.

Figure 18: *Happy Victims*, **Volume 10, in** *Ryuko Tsushin*, **January 2000.**

been used as a bedroom, with a futon put down before the inhabitants go to sleep and folded up when they wake in the morning. Traditionally, the futon would be stored in this same space, although the Happy Victim has converted the storage space into a wardrobe for her Jean Paul Gaultier clothes. As the photograph on the left of the double-page spread shows, this wardrobe is packed with products, although the room looks minimalistic when it is closed (as shown by the photograph on the right).

Daniels suggests that traditional Japanese homes are cluttered and contain many objects. Living in the same home for many years, people inevitably accumulate a lot of objects that they cannot discard, such as gifts from their relatives or heirlooms. These objects are retained not only because they are imbued with social relationships, but also because there is a desire to maintain traditional objects with care.[170]

The way the Happy Victims keep, display and consume their favourite fashion items can be analysed through Pierre Bourdieu's theory of 'Habitus': 'The habitus, is not only a structuring structure, which organizes practices and the perception of practices, but also a structured structure: the principle of division into logical classes which organizes the perception of the social world is itself the product of internalization of the division into social classes'.[171] This process of classification is defined by the practice of everyday life by people from different classes in social spaces. Bourdieu continues:

> Each class condition is defined, simultaneously, by its intrinsic properties and by the relational properties which it derives from its position in the system of class conditions, which is also a system of differences, differential positions... social identity is defined and asserted through difference. This means that inevitably inscribed within the dispositions of the habitus is the whole structure of the system of conditions, as it presents itself in the experience of a life-condition occupying a particular position within that structure.[172]

The 'difference' between the families that Daniels investigated and people living in completely modern houses come from this 'system of social structure'. The interesting aspect of Bourdieu's argument for Tsuzuki's subjects is that 'class differentiation'

---

[170] Daniels, p.204.

[171] Bourdieu, p.170.

[172] Bourdieu, p.172.

emerges not simply from occupation or income, but from consumption habits: what do people wear, what do they eat, what kind of sport do they do? The people researched by Daniels did not live in Tokyo, but in detached houses in western Japan. By contrast, the majority of those captured by Tsuzuki's lens live in small rented flats in central Tokyo. The things that these people consume, the way that they consume them, and the way in which they preserve them in their homes, all clearly demarcate Tsuzuki's subjects from Daniels's case studies.

HOME AS A CURATORIAL SPACE

With regards to the habitus of the Happy Victims (of whom Ishibashi is an extreme example), their consumer goods have been accumulated and displayed, and may therefore be seen as some kind of future inherited objects. Viewed in this light, many of the Happy Victims act as curators in their own homes, conserving their fashion items as part of some future heritage.

The previous chapter addressed the notion of the collector, but this section will analyse the accumulation of objects in modern homes, in contrast to objects accumulated in traditional ones. Ishibashi, for example, has accumulated objects not because they are gifts or heirlooms, but because they are what he loves and so he purchased them. His home does not have any historical lineage because his stay there is temporary (he rents his studio flat), and it is therefore less cluttered compared to the houses in Daniels's text.

Further to this point, Igor Kopytoff's essay 'The cultural biography of things: commoditization as process' is a good source for understanding the commoditisation and de-commoditisation of things. Kopytoff says:

> From a cultural perspective, the production of commodities is also a cultural and cognitive process: commodities must be not only produced materially as things, but also culturally marked as being a certain kind of thing. Out of the total range of things available in a society, only some of the same thing may be treated as a commodity at one time and not at another. And finally, the same thing may, at the same time, be seen as a commodity by one person and as something else by another.[173]

In relation to this, Ishibashi was obsessed with Comme des Garçons until 1995, when he happened to discover Maison Martin Margiela ⑩ in a department store. He was fascinated by Margiela's creations, selling or giving away most of his Comme des Garçons collection because he believed it would be rude to the two designers if he ever mixed their work.[174] Prior to his discovery of Margiela, Ishibashi had effectively branded himself with Comme des Garçons. As long as he thought that Comme des Garçons items were appropriate to him, he consumed them. However, as soon as he regarded them as being no longer appropriate to his life, he disposed of his entire collection. Ishibashi then began to identify with Margiela's items instead, collecting them with meticulous care and preserving them in his room. This is what Kopytoff means by 'cognitive process'. These fashion items are not only material

---

[173] Igor Kopytoff, 'The cultural biography of things: commoditization as process' in *The Social Life of Things*, edited by Arjun Appadurai, (New York: Cambridge University Press, 1986), p.64.

[174] Tsuzuki, *Happy Victims*, Volume 48, *Ryuko Tsushin* (Tokyo: INFAS Publications,), p.150.

products, but are also defined by each individual's relationship with them. 'A certain kind of thing' is generally regarded by the owner as an available and valuable commodity for a certain period of time.

Ishibashi's extreme care for Margiela's items, which I described in Chapter One, brings me to Kopytoff's idea of 'future collectibles'. Kopytoff chooses examples such as old beer cans and books 'worthy of being collected' by being 'moved from the sphere of the singularly worthless to that of the expensive singular'.[175] According to Kopytoff, these items are 'sacralised' due to 'the span of time separating one from one's grandparents' generation'.[176] Kopytoff goes on to say:

> As one makes them more singular and worthy of being collected, one makes them valuable, they acquire a price and become a commodity and their singularity is to that extent undermined. This interpenetration within the same object of commodity principles and singularisation principles is played upon by firms specialising in manufacturing what might be called 'future collectibles'.[177]

What is going to happen to Ishibashi's Margiela collection a century from now? It is possible that his entire collection will be valuable because of the story behind it. We could, for instance, 'sacralise' his collection and make his small studio flat into a museum by de-commoditising the collection and making its constituent items priceless because of the collection's 'singularity'. It

---

[175] Kopytoff, p.80.

[176] Kopytoff, p.80.

[177] Kopytoff, p.81.

is worth noting that Ishibashi told me that he was going to consume Margiela's items for the rest of his life.[178]

We do, however, need to consider young Japanese people's lifestyles in modern dwellings. Out of the roughly 90 people in Tsuzuki's series, 80 were single. This is a small sample, but the high proportion of single people preferring to delay marriage – both men and women – is notable.

THE JAPANESE FAMILY BREAKS DOWN: FROM NUCLEAR FAMILY TO INDIVIDUALS

Daniels describes family houses that possess a certain traditionalism in how they treat objects and the social roles of their inhabitants. On the other hand, the inhabitants that Tsuzuki captured were young singles, perhaps suggesting that some of the strictures of the family may be breaking down in Japanese society – is it becoming a society of individuals? Among the roughly 90 people published in *Happy Victims*, 30 were single men and 50 single women. Those singles seemed to be happy, however. Does this suggest a wider social acceptance of a new lifestyle, or are we just observing a small community?

In their book 'Changing Generations in Japan Today', anthropologists Gordon Matthews and Bruce White address this problem, pointing out that there is a generational conflict between elderly and young Japanese people who possess different views on life. Since Japan's economy began growing in the postwar years, the nation's changing social situation has caused a 'generation gap'

---

[178] Ishibashi, personal interview.

in which elderly people are described by young people as 'inflexible', whereas young people are in turn regarded as 'inconsiderate' or 'selfish'.[179] Even though generational tension is not new to Japan, Matthews and White argue that many young Japanese people are now 'choosing not to enter the adult social order: not to hold stable jobs, as did their fathers, or to marry and have families, as did their mothers, but to follow paths of their own choosing'.[180] This is largely due to economic stagnation following the bubble economy of the late 1980s. Matthew and Bruce go on:

> In tandem with the delegitimisation of the adult Japanese social order over the past decade of economic downturn and social malaise, there is a pluralisation of values taking place. Because 'the adult social order' can no longer claim success, other, alternative paths to adulthood are opening up. Today, one need not necessarily marry and have children, or work for a big company; and even if one does, one can, more than in the past, have a degree of latitude in how one lives.[181]

Nowadays, young people have much less of a guarantee of lifetime employment, even if they graduate from a top university. This has led to the increase of Freeter in the early 2000s, not all of whom are skilled in any particular field and who do not want (or cannot, due to the economy) take a full-time job.[182] Freeters' jobs are varied – they may work as cashiers for convenience stores; for

---

[79] Gordon Matthews and Bruce White, 'Changing Generations in Japan Today' in *Japan's Changing Generations: Are young people creating a new society?* (London: Routledge Curzon, 2004), p.1.

[80] Matthews and White, p.2.

[81] Matthews and White, p.8.

[82] Matthews and White, p.6.

delivery services; at construction sites; or wait on tables. They do not have to be qualified in a particular field, nor do they need high-level educational qualifications. They may not always enjoy their jobs, but they do them regardless in order to pay their bills. Few Freeters work for their employer for their whole life, and their employers would not expect them to. Freeters move on, employers hire new people. Shifts can be flexible and, in this way, some Freeters can secure themselves financially while having more flexibility to work on passion projects such as forming a band, training as an athlete or dancer, writing a novel, designing a website, and so forth. Some of them can also earn an income from these passion projects, which may eventually become full-time employment.

However, the corollary of such freedom is the fact that Freeters are not necessarily in stable employment. They cannot easily build up savings, may not have pensions, and do not enjoy the protections provided by permanent employment. Being a Freeter has become less popular after numbers peaked in 2003 (when there were 2.2 million Freeters). According to *Nippon.com*, which is run by The Nippon Communications Foundation in Tokyo, the number of Freeters has continued to dip, falling to 1.4 million in 2019 as recorded by the labour survey of the Ministry of Internal Affairs and Communications.[183]

Some of the subjects of *Happy Victims* were Freeters. One woman (Figure 19) worked as a waitress in a café in a record company's building. Through this job, she met staff from the label and got a job representing a rock band – her dream role. According to

---

[183] The Nippon Communications Foudation, *https://www.nippon.com/en/japan-data/h00655/more-young-japanese-finding-steady-jobs.html?cx_recs_click=true*, (accessed on 28 September 2020).

Figure 19: *Happy Victims* Volume 74, in *Ryuko Tsushin*, July 2005.

the accompanying text, she had not had a day off work for four months and had been working the night before the photoshoot, only getting home around noon. Because music was her passion (we can see the little piano in her room), she enjoyed her job.[184] Since becoming a teenager, she had been obsessed with the fashion brand X-Girl, taking a five-and-a-half hour bus trip (one-way!) to visit its store in Harajuku.[185] It is hard to imagine that she would have felt it was important to get married anytime soon.

---

[184] Tsuzuki, *Happy Victims*, Volume 74, *Ryuko Tsushin* (Tokyo: INFAS Publications, October 2002), p.143.

[185] Tsuzuki, p.143.

Japan is still a hierarchical society in terms of education —[186] people who graduate from a top university are more likely to be employed by established corporates than those who do not. However, there are now more young people than ever questioning the standard paths constructed by their parents' generation, and thereby enjoying a freedom that past generations never had – although young people are simultaneously subject to a precariousness that past generations were perhaps not.[187]

Another way in which a generational gap has emerged in Japan is through the growing opportunity for women to be independent. In their text 'Mothers and unmarried daughters', Lynne Nakano and Moeko Wagatsuma discuss how there is a generational change between women in their fifties and sixties who are family-orientated, and those in their twenties and thirties: 'this view of generational difference is widespread, although surveys show that the shift to later marriages has been gradual – the average age of first marriage for women has risen from 24.7 in 1975 to 27.0 in 2000'.[188] According to *Nippon.com*, that average age had risen to 29.6 by 2019.[189]

Given the social context of the immediate postwar period, many women had thought (and would likely still do so) that women's happiness could only be secured by early marriage and

---

[186] Clammer, p.5.

[187] Matthews and White, p.4.

[188] Lynne Nakano and Moeko Wagatsuma 'Mothers and their unmarried daughters' in *Japan's Changing Generations: Are young people creating a new society?*, (London: Routledge Curzon, 2004), p.137.

[189] The Nippon Communications Foudation, *https://www.nippon.com/en/japan-data/h00759/*, (accessed on 28 September 2020).

having children. Subsequent generations, however, have been subject to fewer economic constraints – they are less likely to have had to give up higher education or career development as a result of financial problems or pressure from their parents. Thanks to the economic growth Japan experienced after the 1970s, many parents can afford to fund their daughters (who were previously sidelined in favour of sons) through full-time education such as four-year university programmes, or higher levels such as MAs and PhDs.[190]

The 1986 Equal Employment Opportunity Law was a historic moment for women's employment in Japan. According to Merry White in her essay 'Women and Social Change in Japan', 'this act stipulates equal access and pay for women and men in comparable work'.[191] This law was revised two years later to remove restrictions on both women's overtime and work that had previously been considered dangerous to women's health and safety.[192] White continues in light of changes to women's employment in the 1990s:

> Most women are employed in the service industries, followed by wholesale/retail and restaurant industries and manufacturing... Reflecting new choices in educational training, women also are becoming engineered and architects, previously all-male occupations. However, only 1 percent of managers are female, and 60 percent of these women are single.[193]

---

[190] Nakano and Wagatsuma, p.137.

[191] Merry White, 'Women and Social Change in Japan' in *Women's Employment in Japan*, (Richmond: Curzon, 2002), p.187.

[192] White, p.187.

[193] White, p.188.

Today, Japanese women are more independent than their forebears in the 1950s. Since the 1990s, 'employees now outnumber housewives who stay at home, and the trend is not likely to reverse'.[194] Women's growing independence is thanks to changes in Japanese society's perceptions of marriage; the stronger economy enjoyed by nuclear families in postwar Japan; higher educational standards for women; and better employment opportunities, even though it is important to note that the gender wage gap remains. These changes have been interwoven with an increase in Freeters, who prefer (or who may have no choice) not to be involved in full-time or life-time employment. Japanese society has been shifting towards Western individualism.

All the factors discussed in this book are, to go back to what Sontag says in *Where The Stress Falls,*[195] what 'lies just outside the visual field' of the *Happy Victims* photographs. Obsession; collecting; solitude; traditional as opposed to modern dwellings; gender; public and private space; class; home decoration; taste; the extension of single life; and the emergence of Freeters. We can imagine and analyse all of this by observing Tsuzuki's photographs and their depiction of Japan's consumption of fashion. In her book *On Photography*, Sontag says that 'Photographs, which turn the past into a consumable object, are a short cut. Any collection of photographs is an exercise in Surrealist montage and the Surrealist abbreviation of history'.[196] Tsuzuki's photographs not only show

---

[194] White, p.188.

[195] Susan Sontag, *Where The Stress Falls*, (London: Jonathan Cape, 2002), p.144.

[196] Sontag, *On Photography*, (New York, Farrar, Straus and Giroux, 1977), p.68.

young people in their small rooms cluttered with fashion items, but are also 'the Surrealist abbreviation of the history' of the Japanese economy. Sontag defines the surreal by saying that 'As if only by looking at reality in the form of an object - through the fix of the photograph - is it really real, that is, surreal'.[197]

Tsuzuki's photographs of Tokyo's fashion-obsessed still exist – they prove that the fanatic consumption of the 1990s to 2000s happened. Now, in 2020, looking at these photographs again while I wrap up my final chapter, they all look 'surreal' to me.

---

[197] Sontag, p.80.

Conclusion
The media influences consumption, consumption reflects the media

CONSUMPTION REFLECTS PERSONAL IDENTITY

While the consumption of around 90 fashion obsessives is hardly significant in statistical terms, it is worth asking whether the Happy Victims constitute a barometer of consumption patterns in Japan since the late 1980s.

In the conclusion to this book, I will address the following questions: to what extent do the Happy Victims constitute exceptions to Japanese consumption or do they conform to wider patterns in Japanese lifestyles? Should the Happy Victims be seen as the byproduct of economic changes or shifting social patterns? What is the status of these Happy Victims in Japanese culture? And how has fanatic fashion consumption changed over the period between the 1990s when Tsuzuki started his project and 2006 when it ended? Are they merely followers of fashion, or should we learn a lesson from the way in which Otaku culture has been characterised in terms of cultural activities that are productive of new social relations and new identities?

Tsuzuki's photographs sketched and investigated a variety of factors which have flourished in Japan since the late 1980s: fashion, consumption, and youth culture expressed through individualism. Following the bubble economy, young Japanese people have experienced a new type of consumption. The variety of products available to them has grown, as has the information available for making choices about lifestyles they may wish to follow. The Happy Victims are a byproduct of this. They are exceptional consumers only in the sense that they represent the extreme end of a wide phenomenon. Collecting items from a single brand while living in a small apartment may represent an unbalanced form of economic life, but it is still one based on patterns found throughout Japan.

The Happy Victims' occupations and lifestyles are indicative of social change. Few of the Happy Victims are salarymen and many are self-employed. Most are single. Most enjoy their lives and their obsession with a particular fashion brand. It is likely that they delayed marriage because they were independent in terms of both their income and accommodation: they seemed 'happy' with their lives and didn't need or want to alter it.

This idea can be developed a little further with the support of Clammer, who has written about the forms of status acquired through consumption practices. Writing about contemporary consumption practices in Japan, Clammer notes how considerations of 'taste' have entered into both consumption and cultural production throughout history:

> Shopping is not merely the acquisition of things: it is the buying of identity. This is true of all cultures where shopping takes place, and the consumption even of 'necessities' in situations where there is some choice reflects decisions about self, taste, images of the body and social distinctions.[198]

We need to wear clothes and so they are, in a sense, 'necessities'. However, for the Happy Victims they were purchasing something more than a necessity – they were not only buying their garments because they loved a brand, but because they also wanted to 'buy their identity' which could be empowered by fashion. They presumably wanted to be seen as people of good taste, to hear things

---

[198] John Clammer, *Contemporary Urban Japan*, (Massachusetts: Blackwell Publishers Inc.), p.68.

like 'I like your coat – it suits you!' or 'I love your style!'. Clammer makes this point in the context of an argument in which he asserts that, until recently, material culture as focused on consumption in Japan has not been sufficiently addressed in the field of anthropology and sociology.[199]

New consumption habits emerged during the bubble economy, during which consumer choices were based on quantity rather than rigorous aesthetic. After the economic downturn, this pattern was reversed: consumers were still as obsessed with consuming, but had to exercise rigid control over what they consumed. This new pattern of reduced consumption was the result of wider structural changes in employment practices and reduced incomes. However, the essential element that drove consumers to make their choices – the influence of the media and the experience of retail shopping – remained unchanged.[200]

In photographing the Happy Victims and recording their consumption practices, Tsuzuki's intention was to separate them from the general consumers that Clammer discusses. Tsuzuki comments that the Happy Victims tended to have a small and limited social network which revolved around their own particular obsessions. This is markedly different from Clammer's consumers, whose social networks are not restricted by narrow consumer choices.

What gives the Happy Victims 'status'? Is it achieved through their consumption of goods, or through their adoption of an identity which had already been validated by magazines? As demonstrated in this book, it is both. The mass consumption of in-

---

[199] Clammer, p.7.

[200] Clammer, p.7.

formation via magazines is certainly applicable to the Happy Victims – even with the proliferation of social media, magazines in Japan remain a useful source for acquiring information about new shops and products.

Consumption leads people to strive for status by acquiring cultural capital, and by displaying and exchanging materials. For the Happy Victims, status-striving is connected to the acquisition of seasonal, limited, exclusive or anniversary items from their favourite brand. Because the Happy Victims are specialist consumers, they feel compelled to excel above all others in the acquisition of goods from their chosen brand, as well as through the acquisition of special products. As a result, their identities are differentiated from others. They feel proud to have been featured in Tsuzuki's series and it is likely that they were observed by others with a 'jealousy complex'. The *Happy Victims* were not merely following a trend. Rather, they produced their identity by selecting and acquiring materials independently. They branded themselves by wearing a single fashion brand and showing it to others. As participatory consumers such as Otaku, the Happy Victims are actors and progenitors in Tokyo's street and fashion culture.

A DOUBLE MEANING AND THE UNIFICATION OF TRENDINESS AND OTAKU

During the bubble economy, two types of obsessive youth culture emerged – a double meaning of cool or trendiness on the one hand, as opposed to the nerdy and antisocial Otaku on the other.[201] The

---

[201] Hara, p.75.

Miyazaki murders highlighted the existence of Otaku in the media, a hitherto unseen social phenomenon. The media gave significance to the murder, constructing a negative identity for Otaku throughout Japan. The term was widely used in a pejorative sense to discriminate against Otaku as nerdy introverts who were dangerous to society. In contrast to Otaku, 'trendy' people in this period were characterised as attractive because they were seen as taste-makers embodying new trends, which people could read about in magazines.

Since the 1990s, Otaku culture has reached beyond its stereotype and been redefined in the media as trendy. The media in Japan is a medium in which certain cultural forms are absorbed, transformed and converted into the mainstream. From the margins of culture, Otaku was taken up by the media and converted into the mainstream. Once discovered and promoted by the media, it was adopted by fashionistas and quickly spread throughout Japan.

It was not only magazines that contributed to the cultural transformation of Otaku, but also the rise of popular usage of the internet. Otaku, many of whom had been involved in the development of technology for personal computers, were endemic in the development of the internet. Their primary method of communication was online, sharing information and knowledge via bulletin and message boards and chat rooms, posting photographs, songs and videos to distribute their culture. Through their participatory consumption, creating and sharing products, their knowledge and culture has spread not only throughout Japan but also around the world through the global network of the internet.

Magazines, and especially the internet, have blurred the boundaries between trendy and Otaku. Otaku people have become a model of creativity by consuming, accumulating and sharing knowledge and experiences. This theme also relates to the finale of this book, the end of Tsuzuki's *Happy Victims* series in *Ryuko Tsushin*. Faced with falling sales in a crowded market, the magazine re-launched in September 2006, cutting the series as part of its redesign, before being discontinued as of January 2008.

  The re-launch of the magazine and the end of the *Happy Victims* series, followed by the discontinuation of the title, perhaps points to a new era of consumption practices. Again, Otaku seem to be leading the way. In our new environment based on participatory consumption, people are increasingly able to construct a new form of social order, new social networks and new identities. Is everyone Otaku now?

Interview Records

With Kyoichi Tsuzuki

<How was the public reaction to your series?>

European people say, 'It is like my house in my youth'. I had my photography exhibitions in Pairs, Mexico City, etc. When I exhibited my work in Paris during fashion week, the fashion journalists were shocked with the rooms it depicted. However, young people who live in the suburbs of Paris may wear a Hermès scarf or handbag with second-hand clothes – it is not dissimilar to Tokyo.

I presume that the mainstream fashion media would never feature this type of culture, because people in the fashion industry merely focus on the luxury field. I also suppose that Tokyo fashion obsessives are not too abnormal, or too specific to that part of the world.

My photographic series was regarded as unique, but this is only because no one had ever embarked on this kind of project in the context of fashion journalism. There are a lot of young people in the same kind of living conditions all over the world. I also assume that there are a certain amount of young people who are obsessed with high-fashion brands, for example, in Hong Kong, Bangkok and Paris.

<Can you give me a general impression of the subjects of *Happy Victims*?>

They are obviously VIP customers of each fashion house. However, they have never been invited to the catwalk shows, showrooms or a new store launch party etc by the brand – those customers cannot communicate with the designer they love, but they do with the sales assistants when shopping. I get the impression that sales assistants are regarded as being the lowest class of the company's hierarchy by the designer or PR staff. Sometimes a member of the PR team came with me to view my photoshoot, and also to meet their VIP customer. This means the PR team have ignored them in their daily work, even though they are the biggest supporters of the fashion house.

The people in my series do not have many friends – they are quite shy and loners. They meet people to communicate with in the shop, or communicate indirectly with fashion designers through buying the clothes and accessories. They are compensating for their loneliness by purchasing items. Socialised people do not need to make friends in the shop as much as the fashion Otaku [Tsuzuki used this term] do.

The reason why they accepted my offer to be photographed and interviewed was that they could not allow another person to show their collection of the same brand in my series, even though they were a bit embarrassed to show their small and messy rooms.

<How would you regard their spaces?>

I have tried to show a sense of privacy in their rooms, even though they configured all their clothes and accessories for the photoshoot. I also focused on other objects in their interiors, because we can tell their character through the items in the room, such as the poster of a musician, action figures from films, turntables or record collections. This is a kind of voyeurism. Some people were shy to be photographed, that's why I took the photographs of them with their face blurred on purpose.

There are few people who use clothes as part of their interior. If one really adores clothes, the person takes care of them in their wardrobe and does not usually expose their collection.

<How was the reaction from the high-fashion houses? Did they appreciate the feature as promotion?>

My series has basically not been well received by most of the high-fashion houses, even though the inhabitants simply show their personal collections [except for Tom Ford, artistic director of Gucci at the time, and Martin Margiela, both of whom are fond of the photographs and published them in their own publications]. Because my work is not high-fashion photography per se, this was never the kind of promotion they wanted to see in the magazine.

I have received some letters from the PRs of those high-fashion houses protesting against my series because it goes against their brands' high-end image. They don't want to see their products in real life – the consumer living with their products in a small cluttered room. This means that high-fashion houses are keen to hide their biggest clients to protect their brand image from catwalk shows and advertisements, not because they want to care about the customers' privacy.

Ironically, this is very specific and unique to high-fashion. The high-fashion houses are creating a fantasy that is far from the reality. For example, fashion models with different ages, heights and body proportions from the majority of customers or people in the street, as well as way too expensive products, are featured in high-fashion photography. Those models are too young to be able to afford the items, and the editors of the magazines cannot afford them either. Why would you bother creating the fantasies? And how many people would understand the fantasies?

<Is there anything to do with the bubble economy?>

Ninety per cent of the population in Japan was not affected much when the bubble burst. The remaining 10 per cent of people, the wealthiest members of society, were severely affected because the change for them was huge compared to young people with much lower income. For example, the change in their income from 8m yen to 6m yen is big, whereas young people's rent of about 30,000 yen a month did not change throughout the bubble economy and afterwards. We did not feel the economy had changed, but we could not ignore it because the media blew up those 10 per cent of people.

<I think the Happy Victims are a bunch of collectors. Can you make a comparison with other collectors?>

There is a hierarchy in the collectors' world. If someone collects literature or classical records, and fill their walls with their collection, people do not make fun of them. It's because the collectors would be recognised as intellectuals rather than silly obsessives. Or, if someone gets a Ferrari, even though it's useless in the Tokyo traffic, people see the buyer as a successful person. Maybe it's a kind of jealousy, a complex feeling.

However, if one is obsessed with high-fashion items and invests huge energy, time and money on them, people do not take those obsessives seriously. Many people would think they would rather buy a house or go to a fancy restaurant instead of investing too much in clothes and accessories. So perhaps clothing collectors are at the bottom of the hierarchy for now.

<Do you think your series represents Japanese consumer society?>

No. Most young people in advanced countries are in the similar situation. They cannot afford expensive accommodation, which is why they share a house and want to buy things.

The good looking interior design magazines are all fakes. Can you see the same kind of interior in your friends' houses? For this reason, many young people were fascinated by *Tokyo Style* and *Happy Victims*.

Initially, the editor of *Ryuko Tsushin* did not want to show people in the series, in order to create similar environments to *Tokyo Style*. However, I wanted to feature the inhabitants so that readers could imagine the size of their rooms. Having a person in a photograph always helps you figure out the size of the space. Also, I was interested in what kind of people were consumers of those high-fashion brands.

I wanted to encourage young Japanese people who live in small spaces. It is not right to judge people who live in a small, cheap space for being silly for often buying clothes and accessories.

<Why did you feature a wide range of fashion brands, even though some were not featured anywhere else in the magazine? Some brands don't have any other link to the title.>

Fashion brands such as Alba Rosa, Santafe etc are more popular than the high-fashion brands. If you focus on the high-fashion scene too much, you become contaminated by it.

With Nagi Noda - a fan of Libertine -

<Do you think Tsuzuki's work is realism?>

Tokyo Style and *Happy Victims* are the same, in terms of offering a real Tokyo documentary. It does not look like commercial photography at all. Putting clothes on the floor in *Happy Victims* is a part of reality – I do not consider that manipulation for the photoshoot. So yes, it is realism.

<Do you think you revealed your privacy?>

I think it could have been an invasion of my privacy if I had to show my bedroom, but as long as I show my living room that's fine. Kyoichi is a friend of mine and I like his photographs, so I told him that I wanted to show my clothes in his series, especially for the final volume. Besides, I am proud of my Libertine collection.

<What does your space represent?>

My room indicates my consumption.

<Do you see yourself as a collector?>

Yes I do. I am also a collector of the Living Dead Doll (possessing about 80), contemporary paintings, Judy Blame's accessories and kimonos (about 50). My collection has a wide range and huge quantity, so I have to stock things in my parent's house.

<Do you use your clothes as interior decoration?>

Clothes do not have a role in interior decoration. They are for human's body, and we cannot appreciate their three dimensional shape unless we wear them. I don't think it is hygienic to display clothes in domestic spaces, because they would become moth-eaten.

<Do you think you will keep consuming Libertine?>

Yes. It is not just a clothing brand to me, I also respect the designer and team. I do not think there is any other brand that makes me as obsessed with it.

<Do you think the people in Tsuzuki's photographs wanted to show off their collections?>

No. I just enjoy Tsuzuki's individual photographic style.

With Yutaka Ishibashi - a fan of Maison Martin Margiela ⑩ -

<Why did you accept Tsuzuki's offer to be a subject?>

I accepted the offer without any hesitation, because I just wanted to show how fantastic Martin Margiela is. This is part of my promotional activity for Margiela in Japan. Therefore, for me, it is not showing off at all, in case some people think I wanted to just show off.

<Can your clothes and accessories be part of a domestic interior?>

Yes. I feel quite happy surrounded by my Margiela collection. Simply observing the clothes satisfies me.

<I read Tsuzuki's text about your care for Margiela's clothes.>

I always keep my collection on hangers. No item is folded up, because I might forget something in order to plan my whole week of styling if I fold the knitwear and trousers up. My entire outfit plan is a two- to three-week rotation, which is always in my head. Maybe I have the instinct of a collector or a fashion Otaku [said with a slightly hesitant look].

    I care about the position of the clothes on the rails. I take care not to expose them to the daylight to protect them from being bleached, and I clean my room quite often. Not a single thing is kept on the floor except for the patchouli jar, because the dust could stick to that thing and my room could become a bit messy.

I always eat out, never in my room, because if I ate in my room the smell could ruin my collection. If I get thirsty, I run to the convenience store nearby, drink on the spot and throw the waste away there.

A long time ago, I quit wearing perfume as it includes colouring, which could stain my clothes. Then I started to burn patchouli oil in my room, which is done in Margiela's shop as well, so that I can smell it on my clothes. This is how much I enjoy Margiela's creations.

<What do you feel about Tsuzuki's series?>

Tsuzuki expresses the individuality of Japanese fashion. His photographs make me wonder whether people are obsessed with a particular fashion brand, or the clothes themselves. Tsuzuki captures something more important than consumption. He also expresses the relationship between people and clothes.

<How often do you spend money on Martin Margiela?>

Right on my payday. I use all my disposable income, except the money for food and the bills, on buying Margiela items. But I also want to enjoy good food, so I put my second priority on eating out.

<Do you store other items elsewhere?>

Yes, I have other pieces in two different places, which are my relatives' houses. I cannot store everything here.

<Do you consider being outdoors as another opportunity to show your clothes?>

Yes, by being observed with my Margiela clothes I can be myself in public. I should behave in a manner appropriate to the Martin Margiela brand.

<Do you remember the bubble period?>

Yes. I am sure that people were intoxicated. We often went to discos, and Tokyo seemed to be flourishing. However, basic lifestyle has not changed dramatically since then. I was much younger when the economy was great. If the economy continues to deteriorate, potentially I can just cut my food budget to invest as much as I can in clothes.

With Misho Matsue - an editor of *Ryuko Tsushin* magazine -

<How did you begin *Happy Victims*?>

We started this series inspired by *Tokyo Style*. By having Tsuzuki's new series in the magazine, in which you see a lot of high-fashion content, the readers would be intrigued. That was our concept.

<Why do you feature a wide range of fashion brands in *Happy Victims*, even though some of those are not featured elsewhere in the magazine?>

That was Tsuzuki's suggestion, because our connection with those fashion houses is limited.

<You have now finished the series – was this the right timing?>

Yes. We could have continued it, but we had to relaunch the magazine because of sales, which is why we had to finish. Also, there are fewer people nowadays who are obsessed with a particular fashion brand. Therefore, I suppose this was the right timing. Actually, many people have started to think it would be cool not to be obsessed with a particular brand.

<How did people respond to your offer to be featured in the magazine?>

They were quite shy basically, but they hated to see other people who had collected the same brand. They would be jealous of seeing other people's collections. That's why they decided to show their collections in spite of their embarrassment.

Making an effort to buy more clothes is an important part of their life. For instance, many people bring a bento box to their office for lunch to save money, or iron their clothes meticulously – these actions are fun for them. Some people work for their favourite fashion brand because they love it so much.

The inhabitants usually became aware of how many clothes they possessed, right at the moment they had a look at the Polaroid during the photoshoot. They were overwhelmed by the quantity they had collected. They don't have this objective point of view in their daily life, so that was a new point of view for them.

<Do Tsuzuki's photographs reveal anything private?>

No. This is not a guerrilla photo shoot. We book an appointment in advance, so the inhabitants could tidy up their room before we visited. That's why I do not think the spaces in the photographs are private.

<Do the inhabitants struggle financially because of the amount they spend on clothes and accessories?>

No. Most of them work full-time and have a stable income. In general, they have no savings but they have a kind of mental capacity to buy clothes as well as support themselves.

<Are their clothes used as part of their interior?>

No. They put their clothes carefully in their wardrobes and don't usually view them.

<What do Tsuzuki's photographs show in your magazine?>

Tsuzuki showed the general and real lifestyle of young Japanese people, which had not been focused on before because good-looking interior magazines used to dominate society. His photographic style is unique in that it shows very real rooms and high-fashion products without asking the fashion houses for their agreement to feature their creations. This is unusual as we have to contact all the PRs prior to our editorial shoots.

With Seiji Kimura - a fan of Cabane de Zucca -

<Do you have any savings?>

No. Since I became a big fan of Cabane de Zucca, I have had no savings.

<You moved house recently. Can you tell me why?>

I now live in a different place from the room in which I was photographed by Tsuzuki, because our clothing archive [Kimura's wife is obsessed with Cacharel, another fashion brand] has grown so much. Rather than downsizing our wardrobe, we chose to move.

<You could have invested more in food, a car or a house. Why clothes?>

I take care of myself. How I look; what I wear. I would not want to own an expensive car or a great house, but have fewer clothes or cheaper fashion items. I put the priority on how I look and am happy with the other things I can afford with the rest of my income.

<Do you think you are a narcissist?>

Yes. As I mentioned earlier, I do not go out in cheap clothes because I am supposed to be seen by people in public. And I look for a space to be seen in, actually. I admit that this is a kind of narcissism.

<How did you accept the offer from the magazine to be featured?>

When they contacted me, I did not want to have the team in my house because I was a bit wary that people would regard me as such a show-off. However, at the same time I did not want to see another Zucca fan's collection. I would have been jealous if I declined their offer and ever ended up seeing that. Besides, it could be the first and last chance to be photographed and interviewed by Tsuzuki, one of the greatest photographers in Japan. I also was interested in how my room and clothes would look in the photograph – from an objective point of view.

<Did you want to show your face?>

No. I thought it was OK if only I could tell that it was my room in the photo, but Tsuzuki asked me whether I could be the subject of the photograph, in order to show the size of my room. I accepted his offer, even though I did not want to show my face [Tsuzuki used a longer exposure to blur his face in the photo. See Figure 12].

<Are you proud of the feature in the magazine?>

Yes I am. My collection has been recorded as part of Tsuzuki's series.

<Do you think you are a fashion Otaku?>

I do not think so, but people recognise me as a fashion Otaku because of the quantity of my clothes and accessories. But I do not care about it so much – it is OK if I feel good wearing Cabane de Zucca!

<Does Tsuzuki's photograph reveal anything about your privacy?>

Yes, somehow. I would not think I exposed anything private if I only showed my clothes, but I think I showed something private by showing other objects in my room. I am a bit embarrassed about this. I wish I could have hidden them, but I respect Tsuzuki's idea.

<Do you think your room represents the consumption of young Japanese people?>

No. When I was photographed I was 22 and already married. The quantity of my clothes and accessories was unusual. I had started buying clothes when I was in primary school. The least expensive item was about 10,000 yen, and the most expensive 30,000 yen. That is not normal for kids.

<Do you think your clothes and accessories have a role in your domestic interior?>

Not at all. I do not want to show my clothes in my space. I do not want to show them off. And I would not want people to say that my room is filled with fashionable items.

<Do you think there is any kinds of social message from Tsuzuki's photography?>

No. I think his photography is not intensive or dramatic. He just describes our characters through his work, including our objects as well as our clothes.

<Did you hear anything negative from the Cabane de Zucca office, given that you were working for the company when your room was published?>

No. It is such a shame that some fashion houses have made complaints to Tsuzuki. If Cabane de Zucca did that, I would stop buying from the brand.

Bibliography

PUBLISHED SOURCES (alphabetical order)

Ariès, Phillipe, 'The Family and the City in the Old World and the New' in *Changing Images of the Family*, edited by Virginia Tufte and Barbara Meyeroff, (London: Yale University Press, 1979).

Azuma, Hiroki, *Animalising Post-Modern: Japanese Society perceived by Otaku*, (Tokyo: Kodansha, 2001).

Barthes, Roland, *Camera Lucida,* translated by Richard Howard, (London: Jonathan Cape, 1982).

Barthes, Roland, *Image Music Text*, translated by Stephen Heath, (London: Fontana Paperbacks, 1977).

Baudrillard, Jean, 'The System of Collecting', translated by Roger Cardinal, in *The Cultures of Collecting*, edited by John Elsner and Roger Cardinal, (London: Reaktion Books, 1994).

Belk, W. Russell, *Collecting in a Consumer Society*, edited by Susan M. Pearce (London: Routledge, 1995).

Bourdieu, Pierre, *Distinction*, (Massachusetts: Harvard University Press, 1984).

Breward, Christopher, *Fashion*, (Oxford: Oxford University Press, 2003).

Clammer, John, *Contemporary Urban Japan*, translated by Hashimoto Kazutaka, Hotta Izumi, Takahashi Hidehiro and Yoshimoto Hiroko, (Kyoto: Minerva Publications, 2001).

Clammer, John, *Contemporary Urban Japan*, (Massachusetts: Blackwell Publishers Inc, 1997).

Craik, Jeniffer, *The Face of Fashion*, (London: Routledge, 1993).

Daniels, Inge Maria, 'The Untidy Japanese House' in *Home Possessions*, edited by Daniel Miller (New York: Berg, 2001).

Evans, Caroline, 'The Golden Dustman: A critical evaluation of the work of Martin Margiela and a review of Martin Margiela: Exhibition (9/4/1615)' in *Fashion Theory*, (London: Berg, 1998).

Fiske, John, 'The Cultural Economy of Fandom' in *The Adoring Audience: Fan Culture and Popular Media*, edited by Lisa A. Lewis, (London: Routledge, 1992).

Goffman, Ervin, *The Presentation of Self in Everyday Life* (New York: Penguin Books, 1990).

Hara, Hiroyuki, *Theory on Bubble Culture*, (Tokyo: Keio University Publishing, 2006).

Jenson, Joli, 'Fandom As Pathology' in *The Adoring Audience: Fan Culture and Popular Media*, edited by Lisa A. Lewis, (London: Routledge, 1992).

Kawamura, Yuriya, *The Japanese Revolution in Paris Fashion*, (Oxford: Berg, 2004).

Kopytoff, Igor, 'The cultural biography of things: commoditization as process' in *The Social Life of Things*, edited by Arjun Appadurai, (New York: Cambridge University Press, 1986).

Kumar, Krishan, 'Home: The Promise and Predicament of Private Life at the End of the Twentieth Century' in *Public And Private In Thought And Practice*, edited by Jeff Weinstraub Jeff and Krishan Kumar, (Chicago: University of Chicago Press, 1997).

Lange, Susanne, 'August Sander's People of the 20th Century: Its Making and Impact' in *Cruel and Tender*, (London: Tate Publishing, 2003).

Lehmann, Ulrich, *Chic Clicks*, (New York: Hatje Cantz Publishers, 2002).

Matthews, Gordon and White, Bruce, 'Changing Generations in Japan Today' in *Japan's Changing Generations: Are young people creating a new society?*, edited by Gordon Matthews and Bruce White, (London: Routledge Curzon, 2004).

Miller, Daniel and Slater, Don, *The Internet: An Ethnographic Approach*, (Oxford: Berg, 2000).

Morinaga, Takuro, *Moe Economics*, (Tokyo: Kodansha, 2005).

Nakagawa, Takeshi, *The Japanese House: space, memory and language*, (Tokyo: The International House of Japan, Inc., 2005).

Nakano, Lynne and Wagatsuma, Moeko 'Mothers and their unmarried daughters' in *Japan's Changing Generations: Are young people creating a new society?*, edited by Gordon Matthews and Bruce White, (London: Routledge Curzon, 2004).

Narotzky, Viviana, 'Dream Homes and DIY: television, new media and the domestic makeover' in *Imagined Interiors*, edited by Jeremy Aynsley and Charlotte Grant, (London: V&A Publications, 2006).

Nippert-Eng, Christena E., *Home and Work* (Chicago: The University of Chicago Press, 1995).

Nomura Research Institute, *The Research on the Otaku Market*, (Tokyo: Toyo Keizai Inc., 2005).

Oki, Mutsuru, *Everyday French*, (Tokyo: NHK Publishing, 2014).

Okumura, Hirohiko, *Theory on Modern Japanese Economy*, (Tokyo: Toyo Keizai Shinposha, 1999), pp.5-20.

Otake, Fumio, *The Sense of Thinking about Economics*, (Tokyo: Chuo Koron Shinsha, 2005).

Otsuka, Eiji, *History of Otaku's Spirit: theory on the 1980s*, (Tokyo: Kodansha, 2004).

Robertson, E. James and Suzuki, Nobue, *Men and Masculinities in Contemporary Japan*, (London and New York: Routledge, 2003).

Ross, Jonathan, *Japanorama*, (London: BBC3, 2002).

Slesin, Suzanne, Cliff, Stafford and Rozensztroch, Daniel, *Japanese Style*, (New York: Clarkson N. Potter Inc., 1987).

Sontag, Susan, *On Photography*, (New York, Farrar, Straus and Giroux, 1977).

Sontag, Susan, *Where The Stress Falls*, (London: Jonathan Cape, 2002).

Toki, Sayuri, *Be A Photographer!* (Tokyo: Metalogue, 1998).

Tsuzuki, Kyoichi, *Happy Victims*, Volume 1, in *Ryuko Tsushin*, (Tokyo: INFAS Publications, April 1999).

Tsuzuki, Kyoichi, *Happy Victims*, Volume 10, in *Ryuko Tsushin*, (Tokyo: INFAS Publications, January 2000).

Tsuzuki, Kyoichi, *Happy Victims*, Volume 37, in *Ryuko Tsushin*, (Tokyo: INFAS Publications, July 2002)

Tsuzuki, Kyoichi, *Happy Victims*, Volume 42, in *Ryuko Tsushin*, (Tokyo: INFAS Publications, November 2002).

Tsuzuki, Kyoichi, *Happy Victims*, Volume 47, in *Ryuko Tsushin*, (Tokyo: INFAS Publications, March 2003).

Tsuzuki, Kyoichi, *Happy Victims*, Volume 48, in *Ryuko Tsushin*, (Tokyo: INFAS Publications, April 2003).

Tsuzuki, Kyoichi, *Happy Victims*, Volume 52, in *Ryuko Tsushin*, (Tokyo: INFAS Publications, August and September 2003).

Tsuzuki, Kyoichi, *Happy Victims*, Volume 56, in *Ryuko Tsushin*, (Tokyo: INFAS Publications, December 2003).

Tsuzuki, Kyoichi, *Happy Victims*, Volume 74, in *Ryuko Tsushin*, (Tokyo: INFAS Publications, July 2005).

Tsuzuki, Kyoichi, *Happy Victims*, Final Volume, in *Ryuko Tsushin*, (Tokyo: INFAS Publications, August & September double issue, 2006).

Tsuzuki, Kyoichi, *Tokyo Style*, translated by Alfred Birnbaum (Kyoto: Kyoto Shoin, 1993).

White, Merry, 'Home Truths: Women and Social Change in Japan' in *Women's Employment in Japan*, (Richmond: Curzon, 2002).

Wilkes Tucker, Anne, 'Why So Personal?' in *Setting Sun*, edited by Ivan Vartanian, Akihiro Hatanaka and Yutaka Kambayashi (New York: Aperture Foundation Books, 2006).

Wenders, Wim, *Yohji Yamamoto by Wim Wenders*, (London: BBC2, 1991).

Yamada, Masahiro, 'Family and Gender' in *Sociology of Gender*, (Tokyo: Shinyosha, 1989).

AUTHORS ANONYMOUS

Brutus, (Tokyo: Magazine House, January 2007).

Ryuko Tsushin press kit, (Tokyo: INFAS Publications, 2006).

PERSONAL INTERVIEWS AND CONVERSATIONS

Ishibashi, Yutaka, personal interview, (Tokyo, 19 September 2006).

Kimura, Seiji, personal interview, (Tokyo, 18 September 2006).

Matsue, Misho, personal interview, (Tokyo, 11 August 2006).

Noda, Nagi, personal interview, (Tokyo, 26 August 2006).

PR director of Maison Martin Margiela, personal conversation, (Paris, 28 January 2007).

Tsuzuki, Kyoichi, personal interview, (Tokyo, 8 September 2006).

INTERNET SOURCES

CBS Boston, *https://boston.cbslocal.com/2018/09/26/apple-1-computer-auction-sold-boston/*, (accessed on 26 September 2018).

Japan National Tourism Organization, *https://www.jnto.go.jp/jpn/statistics/since2003_visitor_arrivals.pdf*, (accessed on 5 August 2020).

Kai You, *https://kai-you.net/article/70630*, (accessed on 5 September 2020).

Index of Maison Martin Margiela, *http://www.martinmargiela.com*, (accessed on 30 January 2007).

Noda Nagi's website, *http://www.uchu-country.com*, (accessed on 1 September 2006).

Tange, Kenzo, Okada, Toshio, Kaihatsu, Yoshiaki, Oshima, Yuki and Sato, Tamaki, 'Otaku: personality = space = cities', Japanese Pavilion at the 9th Biennale International Architecture Exhibition (2004), *http://www.designboom.com/snapshots/venice04/japan.html*, (accessed on 1 February 2007).

The New York Times, *https://www.nytimes.com/1987/04/09/arts/sunflowers-buyer-japanese-insurer.html*, (accessed on 14 November 2020)

The Official Comic Market website, *http://www.comiket.co.jp/info-a/C71/C71AfterReport.html*, (accessed on 1 February 2007).

Ni Channel, *http://www.2ch.net*, (accessed on 2 July 2006).

Kouganji temple, *http://kouganji.com/garden/roji-garden/kutsunugiishi/*, (accessed on 5 August 2020).

www.ingramcontent.com/pod-product-compliance
Lightning Source LLC
Chambersburg PA
CBHW060840220526
45466CB00003B/1180